HOME FRONT FURNITURE
British Utility Design 1941–1951

For Liz and Caro and Bel

HOME FRONT FURNITURE
British Utility Design 1941–1951

Harriet Dover

SCOLAR PRESS

Published by
SCOLAR PRESS
Gower House
Croft Road
Aldershot
Hants GU11 3HR
England

Gower Publishing Company
Old Post Road
Brookfield
Vermont 05036
USA

Printed in Great Britain at the University Press, Cambridge

British Library Cataloguing in Publication Data
Dover, Harriet
   Home front furniture : British utility design, 1941–1951.
   1. Great Britain. Furniture, history
   I. Title
   749.22

ISBN 0 85967 842 3

'This stuff is here for your correction,
Although it fails to stir affection.'

The Cabinet Maker, October 1942.

CONTENTS

Preface   ix

Acknowledgements   xi

Part I

1   1939–1945: 'War Socialism' and the Utility Scheme   3

2   Utility Furniture: Economic Expediency, Aesthetic Reform, Political Ideology   10

3   Antecedents   25

4   Design and Reconstruction: a New Dynamism   34

5   Post-war Exhibitions: Continuing Traditionalism   41

Part II

6   Utility and the Furniture Trade: a 'Totalitarian Plot'   59

7   Utility and the Public: a Misunderstanding   67

Conclusion   80

Bibliography   85

Utility Furniture Catalogue   91

Index   103

PREFACE

This book attempts to illustrate the various ways in which objects are inextricably related to the political, economic, social and cultural conditions in which they are designed, manufactured, marketed and consumed. Utility furniture is an excellent example of this, the result of an extraordinary alliance between politicians and designers in the exceptional circumstances of war.

The book analyses the history of the utility scheme. Since utility furniture came into being in response to a particular historical circumstance – the Second World War – Chapter 1 looks at the implications that the state of 'being at war' had for the political, social and economic life of Britain.

How these aspects affected furniture design is considered in Chapter 2. The chapter also looks at the practice of design in this period and analyses the relationship between the Socialist/designer ideology embodied by utility furniture and its actual appearance.

Chapter 3 considers the nineteenth- and early twentieth-century precursors of the alliance between design and politics and the various aesthetic ideologies that were to influence both the ethical and visual construction of utility.

Chapter 4 examines post-war reconstruction initiatives and the impetus they gave to design as a means of regenerating the economy. Chapter 5 compares the furniture exhibited at Britain Can Make It (1946) and the Festival of Britain (1951), and discusses the government purpose behind these exhibitions.

Part II is concerned with the reception of utility products in general and utility furniture in particular. Chapter 6 provides an account of the furniture trade's response to utility.

Chapter 7 examines the general public's response.

HD

ACKNOWLEDGEMENTS

I am grateful to the following for permission to reproduce published material:

Bodleian Library: fig 5.9 (Per 175 e 271, 1951), figs 7.2 and 7.3 (Per 175 e 271, 1953) and fig 7.4 (Per 175 e 271, 1957).

Design Council: figs 5.2, 5.3, 5.4, 5.5, 5.8, 7.1 from 'Furnishing to fit the Family', 1947.

John Murray (Publishers) Ltd: fig 2.5 from Osbert Lancaster, *A Cartoon History of Architecture,* 1975.

The Controller of Her Majesty's Stationery Office: selected pages from the Utility Catalogue, 1943, Crown Copyright and Public Records Office, fig 2.1 (BT 183/157), fig 2.2 (BT 183/2), and figs 2.3 and 2.4.

The Board of Trustees of the Victoria and Albert Museum: figs 3.1, 3.3 and 5.7.

There are a number of people who have helped in various ways in the course of writing and researching this book, particularly Paul Greenhalgh and Gillian Naylor. Thanks also to Charles Saumarez Smith and all on the V&A/RCA course starting October 1987. For their help with the photography, thanks to Diane Slater at the Design Council, to Sue James at the Bodleian and to Terry Thorpe. Thanks too to Maurice and Cora Clarke and Frank and Vera Batchelor for their entertaining information and hospitality, to Jan Graffius, Julia Porter and all at the Geffrye Museum, to Skip for his help with the technical drawings and to Thomas. Very special thanks to Jon for the use of the computer, amongst other things, and as always to Shane, Maureen and Sean and John and Kate.

HD

PART I

CHAPTER 1

1939–1945: 'War Socialism' and the Utility Scheme

'The social characteristics of the age determine its art.'
Wells Coates

On 3 September 1939, Britain declared war on Germany. Interrupted shipping meant that timber was immediately in extremely short supply, and speedy action was taken to regulate supplies, using the system of rationing that already existed for food.

From the consumer's point of view the thing that mattered most about the allocation of timber was not the quantity of raw material that was available but the use to which it was put. And, for the civilian population, the manufacture of furniture represented the most crucial area of timber consumption. It was for this reason that the production of furniture, and various other consumer goods such as clothing and crockery, came to be organized under what came to be known as the Utility Scheme.

Underlying the scheme was the principle that if raw materials were in short supply, then the government, through the Board of Trade, must ensure the fair sharing out of those supplies or of the products that were manufactured from them. The Utility Scheme thus outlived the war itself and existed through the austerity years of Clement Attlee's Labour administration. The phenomenon of 'war Socialism' was crucial to the spirit of the Utility Scheme. Although the Board of Trade came under the consecutive direction of two socialists, Hugh Dalton and Stafford Cripps, during the period 1942 to 1951, the term is usually used to refer to an ideology as much as this particular administration.

After the depression and mass unemployment of the inter-war period, by the outbreak of the Second World War there was a substantial body of opinion that looked to government to solve, or at least attempt to mitigate these problems through an expansion of its social policy. The situation of fighting a 'total war' (that is, one which, in terms of the overall war effort, involved every adult in the United Kingdom), provided just the basis for such an expansion. The need to control industries producing war goods

Figure 1.1   Hugh Dalton, President of the Board of Trade 1942–45

and civilian goods meant an inevitable extension of state power.

It is fascinating to note that, far from exacerbating existing problems, war actually brought about an improvement of living standards, partly as a result of widening government control. An immediate and direct consequence of war was the reduction of unemployment, which had virtually disappeared by 1941. The need to maintain a healthy workforce (both mentally and physically) to fight the Home Front campaign meant that the government put a great deal of care into social planning and the provision of goods, not just as a cynical way to manipulate public opinion but as a genuine morale booster. That large section of the population that, before the war, had been chronically undernourished, now had an adequate diet for the first time; the introduction of free school meals, orange juice and vitamin tablets did much to facilitate this improvement.

The egalitarianism behind these broad changes in social policy also affected the Utility Scheme and the production of furniture. It was not enough to license various firms to continue manufacturing with rationed timber. The government had to ensure that the public was not fobbed off with shoddy furniture and that the trade did not simply produce expensive pieces for those who could afford them. The best means of doing this was to formulate an exact set of design specifications, the contravention of which would be illegal, to be issued only to those firms that had been granted licences to continue production.

In February 1941 the government announced a programme to produce 'Standard Emergency Furniture' (Figure 1.2). This was to be supplied to anyone who had been bombed out – 'bombees', as they were known – to replace destroyed furniture. Also, in 1941, the utility mark 'CC41' was patented, and this had to appear on every utility article until the scheme ended in 1951. In 1942 the Central Prices Regulation Committee (CPRC), which was responsible for pricing utility goods, stated that utility furniture production should be limited by the Ministry of Supply to just 20 articles, manufactured to standard specifications. On 10 June it proposed:

i   Prohibition from 1 July of the manufacture of any furniture except the 20 pieces in the Ministry of Supply list.

ii   Prices worked out by the CPRC to be applied from 15 July.

iii   'One or two of the best available designers of furniture' to be appointed to work with the Board of Trade to compile a booklet of utility specifications.

iv   Utility furniture only to be produced under licence from 1 October.

On 8 July 1942 Hugh Dalton announced that he had appointed the Utility Furniture Advisory Committee (UFAC) to advise on the design and manufacture of utility; its members were:

Chairman: Charles Tennyson CMG, Vice-President of the Council for Art and Industry, Chairman of the Board of Governors of the National Register of Art and Design

Elizabeth Denby, ARIBA, specialist in low-cost housing planning

John Gloag, ARIBA, industrial design consultant

W. Johnstone, furniture manufacturer, executive committee member Scottish Committee, Council for Art and Industry

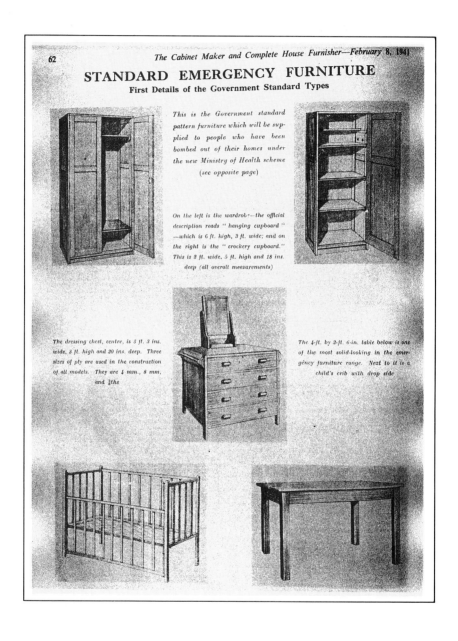

62   *The Cabinet Maker and Complete House Furnisher—February 8, 1941*

STANDARD EMERGENCY FURNITURE
First Details of the Government Standard Types

This is the Government standard pattern furniture which will be supplied to people who have been bombed out of their homes under the new Ministry of Health scheme *(see opposite page)*

On the left is the wardrobe—the official description reads " hanging cupboard " —which is 6 ft. high, 3 ft. wide; and on the right is the " crockery cupboard." This is 2 ft. wide, 5 ft. high and 18 ins. deep (all overall measurements)

The dressing chest, centre, is 3 ft. 3 ins. wide, 3 ft. high and 20 ins. deep. Three sizes of ply are used in the construction of all models. They are 4 mm., 8 mm, and ⅜ths

The 4-ft. by 2-ft. 6-in. table below is one of the most solid-looking in the emergency furniture range. Next to it is a child's crib with drop side

Figure 1.2

Revd Charles Jenkinson, former member of the Leeds Housing Corporation

Herman Lebus CBE, senior partner of Harris Lebus, furniture manufacturers

Gordon Russell, furniture designer and manufacturer, director of Gordon Russell Ltd

V. Welsford, furniture factories manager

E. Winborn, Member of the Tenant's Association of Kensal House Estate.

Towards the end of July, having decided that 24 August would be the date for the final submission of utility furniture designs, the committee approached nine designers for plans. Of the drawings submitted, those by Edwin Clinch and H. T. Cutler, two High Wycombe men, were eventually to go into production. The following month the furniture prototypes were shown to Hugh Dalton for approval and in January 1943 the first utility furniture catalogue announced the forthcoming availability of articles to newlyweds trying to set up home and to bombees through a system of rationing and dockets (Figures 1.3 and 1.4). Although no changes were made to the furniture in this first catalogue for three years, the UFAC remained intact to advise on any problems that might arise.

When, after the 1945 Labour general election victory, Dalton left the Board of Trade to serve as Attlee's Chancellor, his post was filled by Stafford Cripps. In October of that year Cripps appointed a working party to report on post-war improvements in furniture production and it was agreed that the utility furniture programme should be continued while rationing remained. In 1946 a number of new designs were added to the original range and a new catalogue came out in 1947.

In November 1948 'Freedom of Design' was announced which allowed manufacturers to design their own furniture while adhering to the limits imposed for the carcass construction of the original range. In January 1949 the UFAC was finally disbanded and the Furniture Development Council was established to maintain standards and research into further improvements in the furniture industry. On 15 December 1951, the Utility Furniture (Making and Supply) (Revocation) Order came into being, and despite a spirited defence by some Labour ministers, the Utility

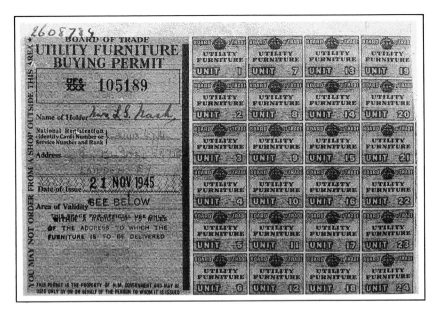

Figure 1.3

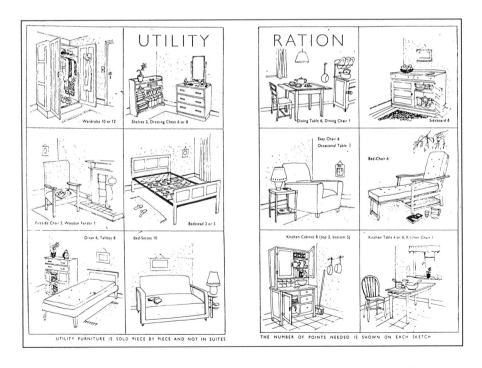

Figure 1.4

Scheme ended on 21 January 1953. The scheme had been one of the most notable successes of the Home Front campaign; certainly it represents a unique aspect of British design history.

CHAPTER 2

Utility Furniture: Economic Expediency, Aesthetic Reform, Political Ideology

'Furniture of sound construction in simple but agreeable design, for sale at reasonable prices and ensuring the maximum economy of raw materials and labour.'
Board of Trade directive, 1942

Of all the industries administered under the Board of Trade utility regulations between 1941 and 1951, the manufacture of furniture was one of the most strictly supervised. Initial ideas about setting general specifications but allowing the final design of the furniture to rest with the manufacturer were soon recognized to be unworkable. Rightly or wrongly, it was felt that relative freedom of design might result in poor quality and thus undermine the whole scheme by bringing it into disrepute. The decision was therefore taken in the autumn of 1942 to invite a number of firms to apply for a licence to manufacture. Six hundred applications were received but, on the principle that every firm must operate as near to full capacity as possible in order to minimize labour wastage, only 150 firms (each employing a workforce of about 40 people) were selected.

Each firm was issued with a licence number which had to be stamped alongside the utility symbol on every item of furniture produced. This ensured that government inspectors could trace faulty pieces back to the firms that had manufactured them. It was punishable by imprisonment for any designated firm to produce anything other than specified furniture.

The eventual appearance and construction of utility furniture were to a great extent dictated by economic expediency. This can be seen in terms of four interdependent factors: the availability of raw materials, the control of prices, the availability of labour, and the organization of factory sites.

It is significant that it was as early as 5 September 1939 that a Timber Control Department was set up, under the Ministry of Supply, to ensure that all industrial consumers of wood obtained a licence to continue manufacturing. Worse was to come. In July 1940 the trade was shocked by the withdrawal of all timber supplies for domestic furniture – a clear indication of the importance that the government was attaching to timber control. Despite this dramatic attack on the industry, it was possible for most firms to continue production using pre-war hardwood stocks and also plywood which had not yet been diverted to the manufacture of the Mosquito aircraft. Then, when the 'phoney war' ended and bombing began there was a slight relaxation of the rules to release timber for essential reconstruction work.

However, on 1 January 1942 all plywood supplies were withdrawn from the domestic furniture industry and its timber quota was cut by one third. Further scaling down of timber quotas according to a firm's size and output meant that by spring 1942 all factories had their supplies reduced to one eleventh of their pre-war consumption. When it launched the Utility Scheme that summer, the Board of Trade informed the scheme's design panel of what was available – that is, what priority users such as aircraft production were unlikely to want – and all designs were submitted on this basis. Thus the brief that Clinch and Cutler had to work to once their provisional designs were accepted was that they should use the minimum raw materials compatible with guaranteed quality. In the end the hardwoods oak and mahogany were used for carcass construction, and hardboard veneered with oak on both sides was the only material allowed for panel construction.

The seriousness with which the Utility Furniture Advisory Committee treated the efficient use of materials can be seen by the many detailed diagrams of the specification booklets (Figures 2.1 and 2.2).The furniture produced under the scheme is devoid of any detail that would require the use of any extra timber. Moulding for example, is extremely rare. From the original range of 22 pieces, only one item – a sideboard – has even the simplest decoration: a half-round shape edging the door panels. Of course, ornamentation does not necessarily require extra raw materials; for example, chair legs can be turned, handles or panels can be carved. But utility furniture had none of this. It was not that all skilled craftsmen had been lost to the services. The explanation had to do with cost.

The manufacture of goods under the Utility Scheme was firmly rooted in the egalitarian philosophy that each item must represent the best possible value for money for the maximum number of those in real need. It is in this context too that the very functional appearance of this furniture must be viewed. Lengthy processes like moulding, bending or carving would clearly have implied extra cost to the consumer.

The UFAC's constructional diagrams (Figures 2.3 and 2.4) reveal how

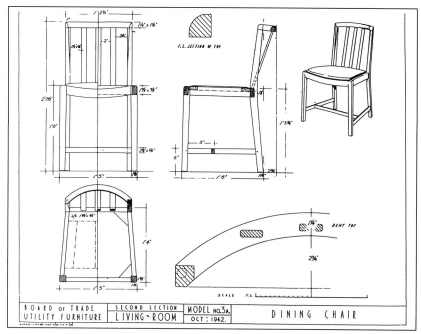

Figure 2.1

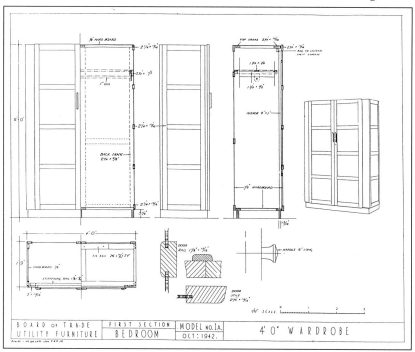

Figure 2.2

Figure 2.3

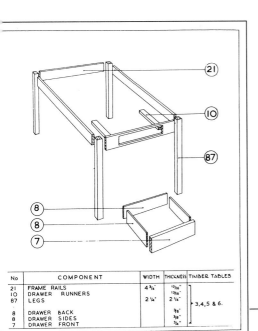

No	COMPONENT	WIDTH	THICKNESS	TIMBER TABLES
21	FRAME RAILS	4³/₄"	¹³/₁₆"	
IO	DRAWER RUNNERS		¹³/₁₆"	
87	LEGS	2¹/₄"	2¹/₄"	3,4,5 & 6.
8	DRAWER BACK		³/₈"	
8	DRAWER SIDES		³/₈"	
7	DRAWER FRONT		³/₄"	

Figure 2.4

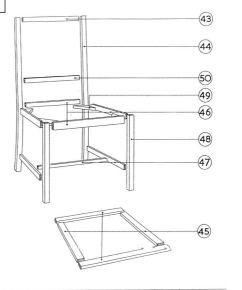

No	COMPONENT	WIDTH	THICKNESS	TIMBER TABLES
43	TOP RAIL	1⁵/₁₆"	¹³/₁₆"	3.
44	BACK LEGS		1¹/₈"	3
45	SEAT FRAMING	1¹/₂"	¹³/₁₆"	3, 4 & 5.
46	SEAT RAILS	1³/₄"	¹³/₁₆"	3
47	STRETCHER RAILS	1¹/₁₆"	⁵/₈"	3
48	FRONT LEGS	1¹/₄"	1¹/₄"	3
49	CORNER BRACES	1⁵/₈"	⁵/₈"	3, 4 & 5
5O	BACK STAY	1¹/₄"	⁵/₈"	3

13

costs were low: each component was quick to cut, each joint quick to construct: butt joints or the simplest mortice and tenon or tongue and groove joints were used. Frames for door panels were also butt-jointed rather than mitred, which would have enhanced appearance but increased cost. (See, for example, sideboard model 1b, 1943.)

The desire to minimize cost also meant that transport and distribution had to be rationalized. The trade was re-structured to allow the manufacture of different pieces by a number of firms in the same zone of the country. Since the sale of these goods was restricted to that same zone public access to the furniture became evenly distributed.

Zoning produced huge changes. Furniture making had traditionally been concentrated around London, particularly in the East End and High Wycombe. The re-organization meant that areas which had previously employed only a few people were suddenly required to engage in the mass production of furniture. Above all, the fact that any firm with the bare minimum of woodworking equipment and production experience could be pressed into service meant that the utility designs had to be extremely simple to cut and to construct. As Clinch put it, 'anybody could make it satisfactorily, and they'd never made such a good job of it, half of the people, half of their lives' (Brutton 1974, p68).

Indeed, the need for reform in the design and production of furniture (among other things) had been much written about and discussed for over a decade. The need to re-educate the manufacturer, retailer and consumer in matters of style had become an obsession during the 1930s which would also contribute to the eventual look of utility furniture.

DESIGN REFORM

There was at this time growing awareness of the importance of the relationship between art and industry which could not be ignored if Britain was to keep up with developments on the Continent. Popular taste in the 1930s was said to be stuck between two equally unacceptable alternatives: endless reproduction, or the debased 'Hollywood Deco' (Figure 2.5) that Osbert Lancaster described so well. In a double-edged attack on mass consumption and Chamberlain's 'Peace in our Time',

Figure 2.5

Lancaster comments:

> It was significant that the Old English fondness for disguising every-
> thing as something else now attained the dimensions of a serious
> pathological affliction. Gramophones masquerade as cocktail cabi-
> nets; cocktail cabinets as book-cases; radios lurk in tea-caddies and
> bronze nudes burst assunder at the waistline to reveal cigarette
> lighters; and nothing is what it seems. On reflection it is perhaps not
> surprising that disaster should have overtaken a generation which
> refused so consistently to look even the most ordinary facts in the
> face. (Lancaster 1975, p.160)

Despair at popular taste was a theme which kept the letters pages of design
journals full to the brim throughout the 1930s and 1940s. Typical is the
exasperation of A.L. Reid, writing to *Art and Industry* in February 1945 on

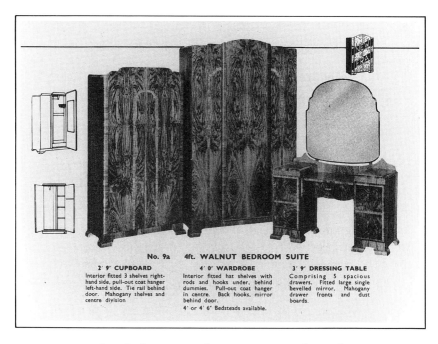

No. 9a   4ft. WALNUT BEDROOM SUITE

2' 9" CUPBOARD	4' 0" WARDROBE	3' 9" DRESSING TABLE
Interior fitted 3 shelves right-hand side, pull-out coat hanger left-hand side. Tie rail behind door. Mahogany shelves and centre division	Interior fitted hat shelves with rods and hooks under, behind dummies. Pull-out coat hanger in centre. Back hooks, mirror behind door. 4' or 4' 6" Bedsteads available.	Comprising 5 spacious drawers. Fitted large single bevelled mirror. Mahogany drawer fronts and dust boards.

Figure 2.6   Walnut bedroom suite from inter-war trade catalogue

'The Anatomy of Ugliness':

> Those who claimed that before the war we were moving towards a democracy of good taste in furniture design had apparently arrived at that state of mind wherein faith triumphs over observation. The windows of the cheap furniture stores displayed evidence that we were still far from the standard that should exist among more highly civilized people . . . To what perverted sense of values do those burr-walnut bedroom suites appeal? (Figure 2.6)

What was Reid's solution to this heinous lack of sensibility? He continues: 'Before one can appreciate good design in everyday things it is necessary to know something of the criteria by which we should judge; the eye must be familiar with what is good the more surely to detect what is bad.' This is, in essence, the argument put forward by each faction of the movement for design reform. Surround an unsuspecting public with well designed objects and they will naturally come to learn the error of their ways. Moreover, the reformers argued, they will no longer be open to exploitation by greedy manufacturers who for the sake of easy profits refused to experiment or innovate, building, in Tom Harrison's wonderful phrase,

'Dagenhams around the minds of the people'. In their campaign against elaboration, the reformers ignored the fact that in the reproduction trade which they attacked so virulently there existed pockets of quality and skill, as well as furniture makers who kept up with the times (Figure 2.7). A honing down and simplification of style were the only considerations that counted for anything. One member of the Mass Observation team put forward the following opinion:

> People have certain habits of design. There are designs which are widely publicly accepted and even liked. That does not mean that these designs are those which people deliberately prefer and choose over all others . . . . I am wholly aware of the abysmal level to which apathy or ignorance in design and taste can go. But it is essential that we distinguish between taste, conscious preference, choice on the one hand, and on the other, habit and opportunity, the line of least resistance and the line of social normality. (Harrison 1943, p.43)

All of the more liberal reformers seem to have agreed with this. Surely redemption lay at hand if only the public could be guided towards making better aesthetic choices. The thing that the reformers could not decide upon, of course, was what actually constituted the 'good design' to which the public should be given access.

The modernists were all for 'fitness for purpose' and efficient design, but they had only a marginal influence on British aesthetic debates – only really involving, it has been said, 'those in the know from NW1 to NW5' (Feaver 1980, p.33). The more conservative faction of the reform movement felt that modernism by no means provided all the answers; 'M. Le Corbusier has an enthusiasm and a remarkable talent for begging the question', wrote the critic Reginald Blomfield scathingly (Blomfield 1934, p.57). Nor would the conservatives take on board the idea that 'the functional', so exalted by modernism, was ipso facto either beautiful or good; 'Big Bertha,' wrote Blomfield, 'could drop a shell into Paris from a range of 30 miles, undoubtedly efficient but unspeakably ugly . . . . And, after all, what might be endurable in a suburb of Paris or Berlin, is quite intolerable on the Chilterns or the English countryside.'

As Blomfield's comments imply, modernism was also rejected as being aesthetically alien to a country in which 'Englishness' (manifested, for example, in the architecture of the Arts and Crafts movement) was so strongly felt. Significantly, the first range of utility furniture was in fact called 'Chiltern' and the second 'Cotswold'.

Figure 2.7

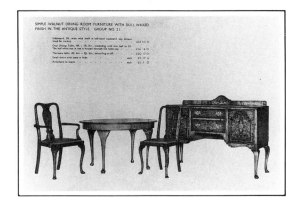

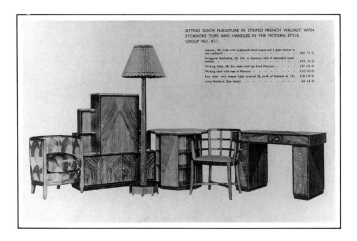

Figure 2.8   Sir Gordon Russell

Gordon Russell (Figure 2.8), the first and most vociferous member of the UFAC, was also a leading light in the conservative faction of the reform lobby. It has been suggested that the striving to improve the average Briton's environment and the philosophy that fuelled this commitment came to an end in 1939. However, Russell's writings from around this time show that this is not the case. In 1947 he stated: 'The 1939 war has been responsible for a remarkable social experiment in the furniture field . . . . In view of the immense scope of the utility scheme it is bound to have a lasting effect not only on the public but on the trade.'

Russell's aims had been clear from the start. In a letter to *The Cabinet Maker* early on in the war he had said, 'our hope is that the committee will plump for sound, plain and functionally satisfactory furniture . . . austerity and utility have useful astringent qualities.' And he wrote:

Side by side with this effort we are already assured of a great step forward in education. Here is a chance to teach the public now growing up. To make them more critical of what is good design, what is bad and why, and so stimulate a much wider demand for better things. (Russell 1944, p.50)

The utility furniture programme was, for Russell, nothing short of a godsend. Here at last was the chance to put into tangible form everything he had been preaching for the last 15 years or more; the opportunity to put into production a design of furniture that would re-educate the public, not through its bombastic modernism, but through its sane, wholesome simplicity.

The copying of forms from a past age which were designed for totally different conditions, materials and methods of production will get nowhere, whereas a knowledge of the past used as an inspiration for the future may be of real value. (Russell 1944, p.50)

Certainly utility furniture cannot simply be described as belonging to the Modern Movement. Visually and ideologically it is much more the embodiment of the sort of honesty in construction and truth to materials so beloved of William Morris, and the ideology that produced utility did indeed have a sort of Arts and Crafts moral earnestness.

Parallels with the Arts and Crafts movement should not be over-emphasized: Russell firmly believed that the salvation of the furniture trade, and with it the improvement in public taste, lay in reaching a true understanding of the machine tool's potential for mass production. He hoped that the production of utility furniture, which was to be solidly factory-based, would provide a testing ground for the application of the principles of mass production allied with uncompromising quality of construction.

The exact extent of Gordon Russell's influence within the Utility Advisory Committee is now very difficult to determine and it is dangerous to ascribe too much to one individual, particularly in retrospect. However, all the evidence suggests that he did exert a considerable influence over the style of the furniture that the committee sanctioned. Certainly, the designs finally decided upon exhibit the kind of no-nonsense, straightforward approach to furniture so dear to Russell's heart. And utility furniture in its simplicity of appearance is quite similar to the furniture that Russell had been producing in the 1920s and 1930s (Figures 2.9 a and b).

The furniture manufactured for the Utility Scheme, eagerly adopted as a vehicle for reform, was the product of an essentially conservative aesthetic, its rejection of modernism reflecting the attitudes of the more paternalistic reformers of public taste. However, it must be remembered that the chief aim of the scheme was the urgent provision of furniture for the needy. The Board of Trade would have been most unlikely to sanction anything visually radical which would have run the risk of being rejected by the public. The coalition government was inclined to act in a conciliatory way towards the public, a fact which had implications for the design of utility furniture. Since the government departments most closely associated with the Utility Scheme were headed by Socialists, it is pertinent to look specifically at the disposition of the Labour Party at this time.

THE LABOUR PARTY AND DESIGN

There are different views as to the effect of the Second World War on British social history. Some feel that it was a watershed. 'The blitz made comrades of us all,' commented *The New Statesman* in 1950, paving the way for a shift to the left in the post-war period. Following the battle of Stalingrad, public opinion too was much less hostile to Communism. Others feel that war merely consolidated trends already present. Certainly, the general trends towards collectivism and a more technocratic approach to government did start before 1939.

Another view, put forward by certain Marxists, sees the post-war Labour government as opportunistic and dedicated not to a profound break with the past but rather, to a sterile, and ultimately, conservative paternalism. It is true, for example, that both Stafford Cripps and Aneurin Bevan had been expelled from the party in 1939, in the one case as a result of membership of the Left Book Club and in the other for sympathizing too openly with the Communist cause in Spain. However, it seems harsh to accuse the government responsible for implementing the Beveridge Report of being stagnant. Indeed, the Labour Party represented a very vital force during the war years, party membership rising from 2,663,000 in

Figure 2.9a   Walnut shaving stand designed by Russell in 1926

Figure 2.9b   Walnut cupboard with bog Oak handles designed by Russell in 1926

1939 to 3,039,000 in 1945. The Policy Committee of the NEC was exceptionally active, particularly in 1944 and 1945, documents being drafted on every major area of social concern.

This is not to say, however, that the period witnessed much of a shift to the left within the Labour Party which, despite its genuine social concern, produced remarkably little social change. Class structure remained as pronounced as ever, most people having no hesitation about placing themselves in one of society's three assumed divisions. The Labour Party that took power in 1945 was essentially moderate and centrist, and this was a reflection of the mood of the British people.

> Attlee's Britain was a conservative cautious land reflecting the reassuring, cricket-loving, down-beat style of its Prime Minister .... There endured after 1945 a powerful civic culture, a commitment to hierarchical and organic values, to Crown and Parliament, to law and order, to authority however it manifested itself, from the policeman to the football referee. It was also a deeply patriotic society, one convinced of its own inner strength. (Stevenson 1984, p.326)

Hugh Dalton, director of the Board of Trade under the coalition government and very much a middle-of-the-roader, was later employed by Attlee as Chancellor. Not surprisingly, the furniture sanctioned under the Utility Scheme and finally given the go-ahead by Dalton was aesthetically down-to-earth and, in this sense, traditional. The socialists' paternalistic outlook, their dream for post-war Britain were thoroughly imbued with a Victorian sense of probity. Correlli Barnett describes their Utopia thus:

> Here was a vision of a garden-city society filled with happy healthy children, smiling mothers, bustling workers, serene elderly souls in a golden twilight of state pensions; all living in houses furnished in Gordon Russell's simple good taste, and, having been equally well educated in a reformed education system, all busy in cultural pursuits other than dog racing or going to the pictures. (Barnett 1986, p.11)

It was entirely in keeping with this sense of well ordered propriety that utility furniture should inherit Arts and Crafts values. The stripped-down simplicity of the furniture was new and, in this sense, stylistically 'modern', but the pieces represented continuity rather than a break with nineteenth-century tradition, and this had implications for the ways in which industry was to be re-vitalized in the post-war period. The social and aesthetic visions of Ruskin and Morris were surprisingly easily accommodated alongside an ethic that owed much to the modern movement.

It is important to note that it was the spirit and not the style of modernism that affected the eventual appearance of utility furniture and the part that design played in plans to rebuild Britain after 1945. In order to unravel the complicated issue of how these two very distinct ideological strands were to shape the role of design, we shall now look more closely at their origins and their influence during the period before the Second World War.

CHAPTER 3

Antecedents

'In the fight against inefficiency, ugliness and
"ornament" masquerading as design each of us is a
missionary preaching the gospel of betterment.'
DIA Journal, March 1917

It is possible to isolate three principal trends in aesthetic thinking during the second half of the nineteenth century. Each of these was concerned with the economic and social consequences of being the 'greatest industrial nation'. Rather than seeing this as a glorious heritage, something which conferred glory, however, it was viewed as being a very dubious distinction, and was very much in keeping with the continuing presence in British culture of the 'Dark Satanic Mills' reaction to industry which dated back to Blake, Mills and beyond.

The first of these trends is represented by the gothicism of A.N.W. Pugin (1812–52). A devout Catholic, Pugin felt that an ordered, civilized existence could only be achieved with a return to a medieval, that is pre-Reformation, society in which everyone knew their place and in which the Church held at least as much, if not more, authority over the life of the individual than did the state. As a Catholic in Victorian England, Pugin had no means of turning idea into practice, but his extravagant gothicism certainly left its mark upon art and design.

Pugin's ideas on morality were similar to those of the Arts and Crafts movement. This, the second group of aesthetic thinkers, based its ideas of morality, not on the chair-leg-covering sexual prudery often associated with the era, but on the dual virtues of honesty and simplicity, which, it was felt, were just as appropriate guidelines for design as they were for life.

Like Pugin, the Arts and Crafts protagonists, headed by William Morris (1834–96) believed that the answer to current social problems lay in re-vitalizing some form of pre-industrial society. A tall order given the spirit of the age, this vision was grounded not in strong religious convictions, as Pugin's had been, but rather in a desire to escape the apparent tyranny of the machine.

The misery brought about by appalling working conditions was also something that concerned the circle of designers whose ideas formed the third school of thought; their solution, however, was fundamentally different. This group of reformers, particularly the eminent educationalist and writer Henry Cole, believed that, if used carefully and intelligently, industry could produce profit which could in turn be harnessed to improve living standards. Archly capitalist, this view was diametrically opposed to Morris's socialism, but it did, in common with the Arts and Crafts movement, advocate the drastic need to improve design standards.

Taken together, the ideas put forward by Pugin, Morris and Cole and their respective followers, were the basis of British design aesthetic for at least the first half of the twentieth century. Later on came the influence of the modernists, and these four groups can be seen as the antecedents of Utility and post-war reconstruction. Attlee and many of the others who were later to make up the 1945–51 cabinets had, after all, been educated at an Oxbridge which, in the early part of the century, was still knee-deep in the liberal arts tradition extolled, not all that many years beforehand by Ruskin as being 'the perfect exercise and knightly continence to body and soul' (Lowndes 1937, p.38).

A less direct, but nevertheless crucial source for Utility and its subsequent role was Ruskin's famous chapter in the second volume of *The Stones of Venice* (1853) on 'The Nature of Gothic'. To cite this as a progenitor of the design of a particular type of mid-twentieth-century furniture may at first seem far-fetched, but any account of utility furniture must look at the Arts and Crafts movement and, since Morris was heavily influenced by Ruskin, at the latter's writing too.

Central to 'The Nature of Gothic' is Ruskin's insistence that:

Men were not intended to work with the accuracy of tools, to be precise and perfect in all their actions. If you will have that precision out of them, you must inhumanise them . . . It would be well if all of us were good handicraftsmen in some kind, and the dishonour of manual labour done away with altogether. [We see] the degradation of the operative into a machine . . . It is not that men are ill fed but that they have no pleasure in the work by which they make their bread and therefore look to wealth as the only means of pleasure.

The key to this was freedom; liberated from the machine, the individual would, ipso facto, become empowered to make aesthetically uplifting objects, beautiful by virtue of the new found pleasure with which they had been made. Morris read *The Stones of Venice* during his time at Oxford in the 1850s. Its influence upon his thinking is not hard to decipher: 'I do not want art for a few any more than I want education for a few or freedom for a few' he was to lecture in 1877 and, after leaving Oxford, Morris

> displayed his opposition to the age ... by attempting to influence people's aesthetic tastes. He began to realise however that more could be done to inaugurate change. He had considered ethical and social problems in aesthetic terms but increasingly he saw that aesthetic questions were inseparable from moral and political considerations – the interdependence of these three branches of life was central in the development of his Utopia. (Cohen 1986, p.6)

Morris saw a return to pre-industrial society as the way to freedom and, specifically, the autonomy of being one's own boss as a craftsman. A highly romanticized, and historically inaccurate vision of the English Middle Ages came to be regarded by the Arts and Crafts movement as the model for their Utopia. Only by returning to a system of work which individuals were free to organize themselves would it be possible for men and women to live honest, simple lives, the beauty of which would inspire the production of beautiful objects. Morris wrote: 'Simplicity of life ... begetting simplicity of taste, that is, a love of sweet and lofty things, is of all matters most necessary for the birth of the new and better art we crave for. Simplicity in the Palace as well as in the Cottage.' (Morton 1973, p.52) (Figure 3.1). Not only does Morris's determination to improve art come across loud and clear but also his desire for the democratization of design through a universal dignified restraint which also becomes a code of conduct.

Utility can thus be seen as part of a tradition in British (and perhaps more specifically, English) furniture making whose design and production is associated with a moral code which calls for simplicity and, therefore, quality. Just as the Arts and Crafts movement believed that honesty – that is straightforwardness – in life was the prerequisite for an uncomplicated, unpretentious style of design, notions of down-to-earth, no-nonsense 'Britishness' became part of the utility furniture aesthetic. Although utility furniture's mass production would, of course, have been anathema to Morris, Edwin Clinch's view of the furniture that it was just 'honest, honest construction' (Brutton 1974, p.86) would have struck a deep chord. So too would Gordon Russell's avowal that 'we cannot say too

Figure 3.1

strongly that we feel that the inhabitants of our industrial towns should not be fobbed off with ugly things because they live in ugly surroundings', (Russell 1968, p.217).

Russell's stressing of the benefits to be gained from good design for industry would undoubtedly have been applauded by Henry Cole. Responsible for the creation of the Royal College of Art and the Victoria and Albert Museum, among other institutions, Cole was a tireless advocate of the need to ally art with industry in order to improve the products of the latter. The chief means by which this should be done, he argued, was education, through either public institutions or exhibitions promoting good design. It was to this end that in January 1848 he wrote to the President of the Society of Arts, who at that time happened to be Prince Albert, making the following suggestion:

Dear Sir,
Having taken an active part in what the Society of Arts has hitherto done for the improvement of manufacture, I shall be thought justi-fied, perhaps, to have matured a plan for extending this object. And

the time seems to me to have arrived when some plan for establishing a National Exhibition should be promulgated and laid before the Society. (Cole 1884, p.116)

This 'National Exhibition' was to become the Great Exhibition of 1851, an event which, although ostensibly designed as an international exhibition, acted primarily as a showcase for British industrial superiority. Cole wrote: 'The history of the world, I venture to say, records no event comparable in its promotion of human industry . . . A great people invited all the civilised nations to a festival to bring into comparison the works of human skill (Cole, 1884, p.116). Also part of Cole's campaign to educate, although it must have reached a far smaller audience than the Great Exhibition, was the *Journal of Design and Manufacture* which he founded in 1848. The journal's aim, according to its editor Richard Redgrave, was to establish 'sound principles of ornamental art'.

Cole's crusade did not go to waste. It was belief in the importance of designing for industry which led to the establishment of a number of the Design and Industries Association (DIA) (1915), the Council for Art and Industry (CAI) (1933) and the Council of Industrial Design (1944), later to become today's Design Council. The DIA in its opening charter announced its aim as being 'the development of British industries through the cooperation of Manufacturers, Designers and Distributors'. It continued:

By encouraging a more vital interest in design in its widest sense [we] seek to augment that high standard of workmanship which is characteristic of British products, believing that thereby the demand for these in the world market will be largely increased.

Sound design is not only an essential to technical excellence but furthermore it tends towards economy of product: the first necessity of sound design is FITNESS FOR USE. (Figure 3.2)

Modern industrial methods, and the great possibilities inherent in the machine demand the best artistic materials no less than the best mechanical and scientific abilities.

This has a very familiar ring. The glorification of all that the machine was capable of was, of course, one of the underlying forces of the European Modern Movement. Although modernism was associated by the British

Figure 3.2   *'Fitness for Purpose' from 'The House, A Machine for Living In',*
Antony Bertram, 1935 (A & C Black)

Figure 3.3

with the dark forces of Communism and with the Left at large and therefore remained largely foreign, in the literal sense of the word, and definitely suspect, that such a dynamic movement should reach Britain was inevitable, especially once Bauhaus refugees had begun to arrive in London in the 1930s. Once in Britain, however, modernism was naturalized, the acceptable elements remaining, with the rest, such as its overt political links (with the notable exception of the Artists' International Association) being ignored or discarded by all but a very small minority.

The straight, clean lines of Utility furniture can, of course, be attributed to modernism's influence (Figure 3.3). Indeed, 'fitness for purpose' was one of the few modernist principles that the British took on board, although the interesting twist is that 'fitness for purpose' can also be traced back via, for example, the Deutsche Werkbund, to the Arts and Crafts movement. Arts and Crafts ideology did much to prime the British for the *thought* of function in design, even though not all of the designs produced by the movement embodied the idea themselves. It is also probably true that modernism instilled into British mid-century design, including utility, an ethic at least as much as a style, the latter becoming a rather watered down version of the original. Fundamental to the modernists was a belief in the machine's potential to elevate human existence. 'In every field of industry, new problems have presented themselves and new tools have been created capable of resolving them. If this new fact be set against the past then you have revolution.' (Le Corbusier 1927, p.13).

This wonderful piece of Corbusian rhetoric should not be misinterpreted, however. It was not the machine per se, but the rationality that it symbolized that was felt to be capable of liberating mankind. The ordered nature of life in the machine age was to be the stepping stone to a harmonious future. The way to benefit most from what the twentieth-century had to offer was therefore to live in an ordered, standardized and integrated environment. Le Corbusier's urge to this end is infamous: 'We must create the mass production spirit. The spirit of creating mass pro-duction houses' (Le Corbusier 1929, section 20). It was as if he believed in some kind of osmotic process by which people could acquire a clear-headed equilibrium from the very walls which surrounded them. Indeed, in this sense, the house as a 'machine for living in' could perform a pedagogic as well as a functional role.

If people were to absorb messages from their new environment, that environment had to be presented in an acceptable form. Moreover, people would only learn from their new surroundings if they were constructed within the framework of a precise and edifying visual language. It was essential therefore that the modern movement formulate a notion of beauty which included clarity, simplicity, rationality and, above all, a complete break with the past. Decoration was not to be avoided altogether but, since it could all too easily involve historical reference or a clumsily complicated and distracting narrative, it was to be carefully prescribed.

Although utility's plainness had as much to do with economic expe-diency as with design according to the principles of a particular visual language, there is a marked similarity of message between modernist rhetoric and the mission to re-educate and reform public taste. If one can talk in terms of causal link between movements across time and geo-graphy, it is possible to see utility fitting into a circular flow of ideas, from late nineteenth-century and early twentieth-century movements, through modernism and back into Gordon Russell's craftsman-like 'vernacular'. Add to this the continual presence of left-wing ideology, from Morris's wish to democratize design to Hugh Dalton's desire that the best quality furniture be available to those who needed it most, and you have not so much a chain of events but a confluence of ideas in which the central themes of concrete beauty of form and spiritual beauty of lifestyle became available to all through the creation of an ordered streamlined society. Only the means by which this Utopia was to be reached varied to any significant degree and it is in this context that utility finally emerges as the successor to the Arts and Crafts vision of the values of quality craftsman-ship, early twentieth-century reforming educational concerns and to Cole's and the modernists' faith in the machine.

CHAPTER 4

Design and Reconstruction: A New Dynamism

'What are the chances of an improvement in the standard of design after the war? There are, I think, a number of factors which make one feel optimistic. In the first place the public feels that there was something wrong with the pre-war world; the very real wish to rebuild better towns for instance is a proof. There is an intolerance of private interests standing in the way of public good . . . we may also note that the war has broken down old prejudices . . . Industry too, is beginning to acquire something of a social conscience.'

Gordon Russell, 1944

The egalitarian ethic that was the cornerstone of the coalition government's drive to maintain morale and which brought the Labour Party to power in 1945 was not merely a wartime mood which evaporated on VE day. In fact, the socio-political climate changed little throughout the whole decade. Optimism, coupled with a belief in 'pulling together', not now to defeat Nazism but to rebuild Britain, seems to have prevailed, despite rationing and austerity, right down to 1951. Although it is difficult to say whether Attlee's government created or reflected this mood, Labour ministers certainly got plenty of political mileage out of recalling the war years' collective effort and contrasting this with the dark days of the Depression.

'War socialism', long before the cessation of hostilities, had included a programme of reconstruction by which the economy would be guided back to normality, and design as a profession had been clearly seen to be vital to British economic life.

The 1930s had witnessed a growing awareness of the economic gain which could be made through the use of design as a prerequisite of quality manufacture. Backed by the modernists' deterministic vision for social amelioration, this awareness was now formulated as a principle for economic growth. The change in attitude represented by this move becomes particularly clear when set against the mood of the pre-war design body, the Council for Art and Industry (CAI).

Set up by the Board of Trade in 1933, with Frank Pick as Chairman, the Council's very name was indicative of the fact that in Britain, unlike the United States, design was still thought of as being an 'industrial art' rather than a professional practice with its own parameters. Indeed the purpose of the CAI was 'to deal with questions affecting relations between art and industry'. In his speech to the inaugural meeting, Pick commented on the need to rejuvenate the British Industries Fair (the the only annual showcase for British design), through the application of 'Art to Industry'. Similarly, in 1935, when commenting on the exhibition 'British Art in Industry', Sir William Llewellyn, President of the Royal Academy, wrote that, 'the right application of artistic principles to industrial production is of the greatest value to the people as a whole'. It was significant too that even those who allied themselves with the professionalization of design practice, like the National Register of Industrial Art Designers, clung to their artistic associations.

The CAI was hesitant in proclaiming the autonomy of designers and diffident about its own role and possible impact. Pick addressed the inaugural meeting thus:

> . . . we are the successors of a good many ventures, both official and private, which have tried to work out a true and proper relationship between art and industry. Many recent steps have been taken, both within the government and without, some dealing with information, some dealing with private questions, some like the British Institute of Industrial Art . . . acting in an advisory capacity only. As I have said we cannot hope to solve this problem, for there are no limits which can be set to it, but we can enquire and investigate in many directions, and after a while may be able to put forward some conclusions of value which would help towards a solution. I suggest that our aims should be modest, our perseverance must be sustained, and that we may be surprised at the fruits of our labours after a time if we make use of everyone who can help us.

No doubt such circumspection was due partly to the fact that the CAI was treading unfamiliar territory and embarking on an, as yet, unquantifiable task. However, as late as 1939, a CAI circulation note, while recognizing 'the value of design in commerce', still used terminology borrowed from the decorative arts to define the activity: 'By design is meant shape, colour, surface as well as decoration', explained the leaflet.

Although much more confident in later life, the CAI's apparent trepidation to define design as a distinct professional practice with direct relevance to industrial production was never to completely disappear. Indeed as the pace to ally design and industry quickened so the Council's desire to harness and make safe this new force seems to have grown stronger. Reading between the lines of committee meeting minutes it appears to have been for this, probably subconscious, reason that emphasis continued to be placed upon the artistic/craft side of production, once again testifying to William Morris's legacy to British design.

Utility furniture too owed a good deal to the Arts and Crafts movement, as seen in the previous chapters. Writing retrospectively on the influences that had shaped utility furniture, Gordon Russell commented, 'I saw that the Arts and Crafts leaders were trying to bring designer and maker together, in itself a worthy objective.' Significantly though, he added: 'but by insisting that the craftsman should design everything that he made they went a bit too far . . . . It became clear that the designer must have a thorough knowledge of methods of production by hand or machine.' It was in insisting on the traditional values of good quality and sound construction and at the same time, on the importance of design for mass production, that the Utility Scheme provided a link between the CAI school of thought and the emergence in the war years of design as a distinct professional practice.

The post-war government evidently intended to involve itself to an unprecedented extent in matters of design. As Misha Black wrote pointedly in *Picture Post* (January 1945): 'The enforced break with tradition that this war has brought, and a realization of the difficulties we shall have to face in regaining and expanding our export trade after the war, has at last galvanized the government into belated action.' In keeping with the mood of the times (and in sharp contrast to the minimal intervention by the Board of Trade into CAI business), war socialism, and thereafter the Labour government, implemented a programme in which design was handled like any other sphere of economic activity: the profession and its practitioners were now often the subject of rigorous bureaucratic controls, performance monitoring and projections. This had a number of implications for post-war design.

One of the more profound effects of the war was that from economic exigency had grown a desire for a collectivist approach to government in which the state would take primary responsibility for the welfare of its citizens. With collectivism emerged an increasingly technocratic approach to government. The extension of state control that resulted from the Home Front campaign meant a greatly increased need for information about the socio-economic life of the nation, forcing a situation which it is difficult to imagine the Conservative side of the coalition having tolerated in any other circumstance. With Attlee as Deputy Prime Minister and in effect, Leader of the House of Commons, the government threw all its weight behind a push for strongly centralized planning, which was endorsed by the Keynesians in the Cabinet. As one historian has put it, 'the planners were definitely in the ascendant' (O'Morgan 1984, p. 297). Set against this background and the bureaucracy it entailed ('I've never sat in on such a lot of hoo-hah in all my life,' Clinch later remarked), the Utility Scheme becomes easier to comprehend.

The UFAC reflected, on a small scale, the government's way of operating – its rigorous technocratic approach, for example. The UFAC's use of the CAI report on the 'Working Class Home; Its Furnishing and Equipment' of May 1937 can be compared with Beveridge's extensive use of the many social surveys produced in the 1930s: in both cases, the aim was an improvement of existing conditions which was seen as essential to post-war economic survival, and both were examples of well meaning, but ultimately conservative, paternalism. Paul Addison has argued that this approach acted as a smoke-screen behind which no fundamental social or economic changes were ever considered. 'In general,' he says, 'this reform programme

> originated in the thought of an upper and middle class of socially concerned professional people, of whom Beveridge and Keynes were the patron saints. To render capitalism more humane and efficient was the principal aim of the professional expert. In the Second World War the humane technocrat provided a patriotic compromise between Conservatism and Socialism which virtually satisfied the desire of the Labour Party for social amelioration without in any way attacking the roots of exploitation and injustice. (Stevenson, 1984, p. 326)

It is true that 'planning' implied a degree of cautious deliberation which could in no way be said to have been radical. Nevertheless, this attitude provided the basis for an inspired programme of economic rejuvenation, born of genuine social concern. War socialism, Keynesianism and technocracy established an egalitarian ethic and set of institutions in the years immediately following the war which were only finally eroded in the 1980s.

Despite the enormous wartime drive to facilitate central planning, it was in the post-1945 period that technocracy reached its apotheosis. By now the socialists were at the helm and the work of the Reconstruction Committee, backed by Attlee and Herbert Morrison, was to prove pivotal to the design history of this period. It was at this point that a belief in design as a significant economic activity appears finally to have been formulated.

Planning extended into all areas of economic and social life and since, during the war, design under the Utility Scheme had come to represent a ready-made programme of government intervention, it is hardly surprising that the planners were able to extend their reach into this realm of activity too.

Although not a government venture, a key step in this direction had been made as early as 1942 with the setting up of the Design Research Unit, which became virtually the first body in the country to talk of 'industrial design'. The unit operated on the principle that research into current design practice in the industrial sector would lead to products being used more efficiently, reduce production costs, give the consumer better value and boost sales. Of course, with the prescribed designs of the Utility Scheme, the unit could not do much more than build up a fund of knowledge for the post-war period. But this knowledge was of great interest to the government. If the problems of the 1920s were not to recur, it was crucial that the coalition make contingency plans against employment, commodity and housing shortages. Thus, on 1 February 1943, Hugh Dalton announced to the newly formed Reconstruction Committee: 'I have made arrangements for the intensified study of post-war problems. Consultations are now going forward systematically, both with certain national bodies . . . and also with particular industries.' Overtures of this nature were, it seems, signs of a new dynamism at the Board of Trade. However well intentioned the Council for Art and Industry had been, it had always subscribed to the principle of government from above, seldom stooping to act together with manufacturers.

Further proof of the Board's new vigour came in the form of suggestions that sponsorship from relevant national bodies be attained for articles of good, innovative design. This, it was felt, would enable them to be shown in teaching establishments and to the public at large and thus heighten public awareness of industry's post-war potential. No longer was the state's participation in design matters to be purely advisory. Active promotion and direct contact with both producer and consumer were the Board of Trade's new policies. Clearly the CAI's days were numbered.

In the early months of 1944, the recommendation was put forward that a new central design body be set up in place of the CAI to have as its principal function the establishing and financing of 'a permanent building for the exhibition of products of good design'. In fact, exhibition space of this type did not materialize until 1956 with the opening of the Design Centre. Nevertheless, public and government awareness of industrial design grew and remained strong throughout the period and was to prove a vital force in making the design profession an integral part of the socialists' post-war economic restructuring initiatives.

Central to the consolidation of design as a profession was the Council of Industrial Design (CoID), set up by the Board of Trade in 1944. Its purpose was 'to promote by all practicable means the improvement of design in the products of British industry'. Although the new body picked up where the CAI had left off, the two organizations were very different:

> We must make a sustained effort to improve design and to bring industry to recognize the practical importance of this task. You have to arouse the interest of ordinary men and women and you have to encourage industry to help itself, through the establishment of an industrial design centre.

Compare this extract from Hugh Dalton's speech to the inaugural meeting of the CoID with Pick's equivalent address to the CAI (quoted above). The vitality of the CoID was particularly marked after 1945. A realization of the benefits to trade of close government supervision of standards, as had occurred under the Utility Scheme, together with the urgent need for economic planning, made industrial design a priority for the peacetime government.

By 1951 government publicity for the Festival of Britain could proclaim that the event had been organized 'to demonstrate the British contribution to civilization, past, present and future in the arts, science, technology and industrial design'. The concept of the professional designing for industry was now embraced so wholeheartedly that for a while the term 'industrial designer' came to mean anyone designing for mass production. The

Homes and Gardens pavilion at the Festival of Britain site was designed, for example, to 'show the part that the industrial designer can play in furnishing and equipping the home'.

Although 'industrial designer' became something of an umbrella phrase during the late 1940s and the 1950s, the Utility Scheme experience of direct intervention into design provided the impetus to set up design bodies specific to individual trades. Here again the voice of the Reconstruction Committee is clearly audible. As early as 1943 it stated that: 'The removal of control of furniture production at the end of the war with Germany ... would be disastrous since with a widening gap between supply and demand, prices would rocket.' Furthermore, with continuing timber shortages and the desire to maintain high standards, a system of quality control was felt to be essential, and 'the most convenient form of control is the existing prohibition of manufacture except under licence'.

For this reason the Utility Furniture Scheme remained intact until 1949. But in the same year a new body, the Furniture Development Council (FDC), was established to oversee furniture design standards and to promote trade awareness of the vital importance of quality manufacture. With Jack Pritchard as Chairman, the FDC maintained strong links with the CoID, the mutually reinforcing work of the two bodies becoming particularly apparent after 1947 when Gordon Russell assumed chairmanship of the CoID.

The furniture industry and the design profession in general emerged from the Second World War not weakened by the drastic austerity measures or the removal of autonomy, but actually revitalized by energetic state intervention. Furthermore, both were now ready and willing to prove that war had not been debilitating. The CoID and Board of Trade used exhibition as a way of demonstrating the new potential vitality in design, and this is a dominant feature of the design history of the second half of the 1940s.

CHAPTER 5

Post-War Exhibitions: Continuing
Traditionalism

'Beams of light will pierce the black-out to reveal, against
a vivid background of bomb shattered London, industry's
newest contributions to domestic comfort and con-
venience.'
'Britain Can Make It' exhibition note on 'War to Peace'
section, 1946

On entering the 1946 Britain Can Make It (BCMI) exhibition, the visitor
immediately encountered a display entitled 'War to Peace'. Twenty
recently designed everyday domestic objects were displayed alongside
wartime articles which although now superseded, had in some way
contributed to the current design. There were new raincoats adapted from
materials used for gun-crew suits, and resin-bonded plywood furniture
which owed much to the manufacture of plywood Mosquito aircraft.

In many ways this display characterized the fundamental theme of this
and subsequent exhibitions, through to the Festival of Britain in 1951.
BCMI, the British Industries Fairs and the Festival of Britain all had the
fundamental aim of proving that war had not left Britain economically
devastated but had, in fact, galvanized the country into playing a leading
role in the world market.

The CoID had been formed with exhibitions in mind. Its charter stated
part of its function to be: 'To advise government departments on the
design of goods that they purchase and to be responsible, from the design
point of view, for the goods showing on government stands in international exhibitions.' The concept of holding exhibitions of British design
was by no means a new one, but it was now energetically re-launched. Once
again Britain was on the offensive: 'pulling together', the clarion call of the
war effort, was now reiterated as a means of boosting economic recovery.

In order to understand the government's involvement in post-war
exhibitions, it may be helpful to look at the part played by the Board of
Trade, through the CoID, in BCMI and in the Festival of Britain. To show
the extent to which goods on exhibition were the product of a particular
set of socio-political values and were influenced by the utility ethic, this

chapter concentrates on developments in furniture design.

Writing in 1946 for the Board of Trade supplement to the CoID journal on BCMI, Stafford Cripps, Director of the Board of Trade, said of the exhibition:

Here we are able to prove, by selected examples of British consumer goods, most of them already in the shops or in quantity production, not only that Britain *can* make it – for the war proved that beyond a doubt – but that Britain can make goods that are new, beautifully designed and efficient as well as of traditionally sound workmanship. The keynote of this exhibition is the excellence of British design and designers' convincing demonstration of the importance of design for a rising standard of living; here are the goods which because they are for economic mass production, will enrich the homes and daily lives of each one of us.

It was clearly hoped that design would continue to act as a fillip to public morale. It was important that it did so as rationing and austerity were to continue for the rest of the decade and in any case the government saw no reason why quality goods should not continue to improve people's environment. Cripps campaigned:

At home our common objective is a standard of living. And we must not think of that desirable aim merely in quantifiable terms, regardless of its character, that is regardless of the quality our income can buy. You can have squalor and ugliness even among riches. Neither the maker or the user can get real satisfaction out of ugliness or shoddiness. And a standard of living which fails to give pleasure and satisfaction is a fraud.

Not surprisingly, Britain Can Make It had a strongly didactic feel. One section entitled 'What Industrial Design Means' was intended to talk the visitor through the manufacture of an object – in this case, an egg cup (Figure 5.1) – from conception to production. Attempts to familiarize the public with product design and to establish the profession as something which had the potential to improve everyone's standard of living was to be a vital ingredient at the exhibition.

The educational side of BCMI was also intended to make the public and trade aware of good design as an important means of boosting exports

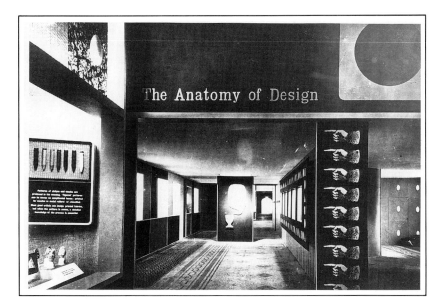

Figure 5.1   The Anatomy of Design section at 'Britain Can Make It'

which would in turn improve the nation's living standards. In doing this the exhibition was fulfilling its original CoID brief. At the CoID's inaugural meeting in January 1945 Dalton had said:

> This is not a new subject but it has a new urgency. . . . On design alone we were threatened pre-war, even in our home dress trade by American importation, and in our glass trade by Czechoslovakia. Examples can be multiplied from very many consumer industries. And after the war, things may well be worse because of the large progress made in other countries, particularly America. . . . We must therefore make a sustained effort to improve design and to bring industry to recognize the practical importance of this task. You have to arouse the interest of ordinary men and women and to encourage industry to help itself.

Even if the government had chosen to be purely cynical, there was no longer, in the post-war period, any need for quality goods to act as a palliative in the maintenance of Home Front morale. However, Britain Can Make It shone the spotlight on the Board of Trade's insistence that excellence in the design and manufacture of goods be brought within the reach of every man and woman in the country. And, if this was not immediately possible, as was seen to be the case in 1946, then exhibitions stood as a pledge that the government was doing its very best to achieve this ideal. For this reason the basic creed of the Utility Scheme – the provision of quality goods for the most needy – remained intact right through the period (influencing the furniture trade even after the establishment of 'Freedom of Design' in 1948). During the war Utility had in part been intended to act as a morale booster and to reassure the public that it was fighting for a caring government. It could now be easily slotted into a campaign which had as its leitmotiv the unstinting effort of the Labour Party to build a brighter, stronger, better Britain.

As the medium by which the citizen's environment could be improved, design fitted neatly into the paternalistic, quasi-modernist view of human need adopted by the aesthetic reformers and by the socialists. The maxim 'good design – good business' (coined by Gordon Russell in 1946), is evidence of the profession's endorsement of the capitalist economy. There was, of course, never any real doubt, especially under Stafford Cripps, that the essentially conservative socialists would build their reconstruction programme into the existing economic structure. Nevertheless, the modernist plea for well designed objects to act as a catalyst in attempts to improve man's environment, and thus, it was assumed, lifestyle, was further justification for using good design as a means of upgrading industrial output.

Typical of the revisionist mood of the Labour Party under Attlee was its awareness that prosperity would not just be the end product but was actually a prerequisite of the programme to raise the nation's living standards. Unless the state's finances were reasonably healthy it would not be feasible to fund the welfare state through taxation. Thus the new administration saw its function as providing the springboard for economic growth in the best Keynesian sense, at the same time committing itself to a policy of actively encouraging the open market and free competition. Here, however, lurked the threat of individual over corporate gain. This dilemma significantly affected the mutually reinforcing roles of the Utility Scheme and the national design exhibitions

Another less obvious aspect of the government's encouragement of good design through national exhibitions was that a policy centred on consumer interest also justified the socialists' drive to establish free competition. It is impossible to say whether this policy was ever consciously formulated by the Attlee government, but as early as September 1943 Reconstruction Committee minutes stated: 'It is worth pointing out that improved standards may increase competition by increasing each manufacturer's potential market.'

The post-war government clearly recognized that good design was a vital ingredient in the recipe for economic success, but the Labour Party was committed to pursue policies which would provide better objects not just for those who could afford them but for everyone.

One of the more eye-catching sections at Britain Can Make It was the series of 'Furnished Rooms' designed with particular families or individuals in mind. Its aim was to promote the idea that design could affect every aspect of daily life and that it could do so regardless of social or economic situation. This is another example of the Board of Trade and the CoID purveying the Labour government's conservative, hierarchical view of society.

Although government-backed initiative to provide a showcase for British design in the second half of the 1940s reflected a far greater dynamism than had been present in this field in the 1930s, the furniture exhibited remained remarkably untouched by this vitality. There were no radical innovations. The best contemporary designs often simply mirrored the more advanced output of the 1930s. For example, the eponymous Ercol chair with its overt references to the Windsor chair and the traditional craft side of manufacture, was everywhere in evidence (Figure 5.2). It is indicative of the aesthetic reserve of BCMI that even the room created for the young architect and his family was kitted out with four of these chairs (Figure 5.3).

This exhibition, and in particular 'Furnished Rooms' seems to have played safe, using objects which could be relied upon to appeal to, if not the lowest, then certainly a middle, common denominator. There is very little difference in appearance between the bedroom fittings (wardrobe, dressing table and so on) prescribed for the working-class flat (Figure 5.4) and those used in the room for the 'single woman author' (Figure 5.5). Nor, indeed, do these items differ much from Gordon Russell's work of the 1920s (Figure 5.6).

It is hard to imagine how else – with its aim of achieving all-round appeal to as wide an audience as possible – the exhibition could have worked. The stylistic homogeneity in the furniture shown must have arisen in part from the egalitarianism of the CoID. The clear intention was

The actual room at the Exhibition, photographed here, was only 13 feet x 9 feet instead of 18 feet x 12 feet. It therefore appears more crowded than it would be. In fact the room divides easily and naturally into the space round the fire and that round the table.

LIVING-ROOM

IN A SMALL HOUSE ON
A NEW ESTATE

Designed by Miss Elizabeth Denby,
HON. A.R.I.B.A.

FAMILY

A young artisan who enjoys a bit of carpentry and is a motor cyclist. His wife, formerly a school teacher. Their baby. His mother-in-law, clever at needlework and embroidery.

Figure 5.2

Figure 5.3

Figure 5.4

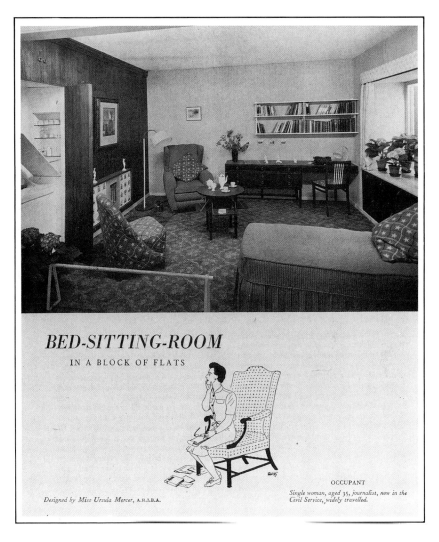

Figure 5.5

Figure 5.6   Gordon Russell boot cupboard, 1925

to encourage an awareness that design could play a part in everyone's daily life and that high standards of design were available to all. If it is hard at first to square this notion of equality with the obvious class statements contained in 'Furnished Rooms', it should be remembered that the entire programme for social and economic reform operated within a rigid class structure which everyone (except a minority on the extreme left) accepted. In any case, as with the design of utility furniture, radical innovation would have produced an aesthetic that would have run counter to the socialists' centrist ideology.

The shock of the 'unBritish' new had to be lessened by a naturalization of design wherever possible and this again meant endowing objects with a quintessential Englishness in the form of references to past craftsmanship, hence the frequent appearance of the Ercol chair at BCMI. Of the furnished rooms Alan Walton wrote in the CoID's supplementary BCMI journal: 'The new rooms are not of static design excluding individuality. They express personal preferences, are sensitive to colour and are able to amalgamate the good things of the past with the good things of today.' In the same journal, Cripps wrote of Britain Can Make It, 'This exhibition will prove that Britain has passed from the years of endurance to the years of achievement and will show the foreign buyer that he can still look to Britain as he has always done in the past for goods of quality, distinction and beauty.'

Whether this was what the overseas buyer really looked for in British design or whether this was just what the CoID liked to think was the case is an interesting question. Yet, in a sense, it hardly mattered. Having chosen to market British products in this way, the assumption of an inexorable link between good design, craftsmanship and traditionalism was at once the reason for, and a perpetuator of, the tendency to shy away from truly radical design. Thus the government's attitudes to design for the export market and the home market were closely related.

There was a keen desire not to waste the experience of the Utility Scheme. Neither public nor trade were to be allowed to return to their old bad habits. Of the manufacture of furniture, in particular, it was felt that Utility had forced the elimination of 1930s reproductive excesses, and while there was no immediate danger of a return to pre-war standards, there was no time to be lost in proselytizing the new creed of simplicity. Gordon Russell, never one to miss the chance to propagandize, wrote of the Festival of Britain, in the pamphlet 'Design at Work' in 1948:

> There is very little time and a full realization of the necessity of a permanent grading up of standards of design instead of a short-lived attempt to produce stunts, is required. If this can be done, then 1951 will mark as great a turning point in our industrial history as did our development of the industrial revolution in the nineteenth century which made us the workshop of the world. (Russell, 1948, p. 15)

It is important not to be misled by the urgency and vitality of this message. Russell's warning against short-lived stunts hints at what improved design was to consist of: furniture design at the Festival was not, with the odd exception, like Ernest Race's Antelope chair (Figure 5.7), any more stylistically innovative than BCMI furniture. Indeed, some of this furniture made a second appearance (Figures 5.8 and 5.9). The main thing that can be said of Festival furniture is that it simply consolidated the 'contemporary style – mid-century modern – which fulfilled CoID criteria for good design' (MacDonald and Porter, 1990).

Furniture design at the Festival was admittedly much simpler than pre-war furniture for the popular market, showing that, as Gordon Russell had prophesied, Utility had had 'astringent' qualities. Despite this, however, the pieces were still essentially conservative; at best they were only a modified form of the more avant garde pieces that had been produced before the war and sold at 'up-market' shops like Heals. Not surprisingly,

Figure 5.7

some of the post-war generation of young designers were disappointed
with the Festival. Terence Conran, who was working as an assistant to an
architect working on Festival design, commented that designers had
thought:

> 'ah, now we're going to be important people in society and to have a
> lot of work' and suddenly we were all out of a job . . . all my sort of
> bright hopes collapsed . . . and I had to start up my own work shop
> and . . . I got a display job at Simpsons of Piccadilly in the afternoons.
> (London History Workshop, 1986)

The stasis in design at this time is further coroborated by other comment-
ators. One wonders whether John Gloag had to do any rewriting of earlier
material when in 1951 he wrote an article for *Design*. In a familiar painting
of a whimsical scene of the craftsman at one with his materials he elevates
the maker to the sort of height that would have been recommended by

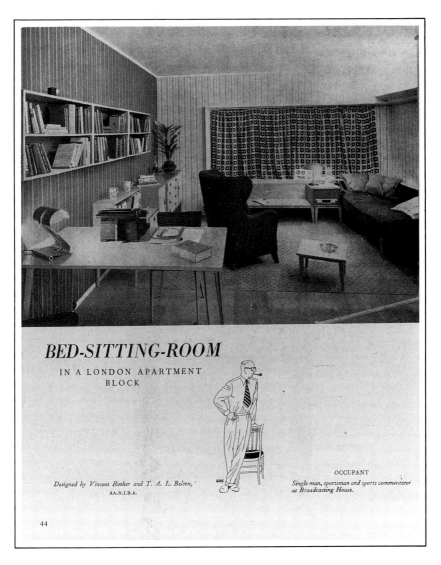

Figure 5.8

Figure 5.9 Bed-sitting room for bachelor girl, 'Festival of Britain', 1951

Ruskin and Morris:

> Furniture designed and made in Britain today preserves continuity
> with tradition, not in form or ornament, but by the way designers
> tackle problems and use materials . . . [Furniture manufacture] may
> be classified under three broad headings:

1 Furniture made in small workshops, largely by hand, by artist
   craftsmen.

2 Furniture produced in factories by manufacturers, who retain,
   generally as consultants, competent industrial designers.

3 Furniture produced in factories by manufacturers who copy,
   adapt or merely caricature traditional or contemporary styles
   and models.

The work of the first group, artist-craftsmen, employs traditional materials and methods of making, and it represents research work in design, which, after a time-lag of a few years, indirectly influences the work of the furniture trade. The work of artist-craftsmen also affects the outlook of industrial designers, some of whom are themselves executant craftsmen.

From the second group, which represents effective collaboration between industrial designers and progressive manufacturers, a recognizable style is emerging that demonstrates by the way various woods and other materials are handled, that the inspiration of the golden age of eighteenth-century cabinet-making still has a breath of life.

It is clearly the spiritual value of eighteenth-century furniture embodied in contemporary styles to which Gloag is referring since he continues: 'Acting upon the assumption that neither Queen Anne, Chippendale, Hepplewhite nor Sheraton is dead, manufacturers of the third group are responsible for innumerable parodies of antique furniture. Such inept borrowing still affects a large proportion of the output of the furniture industry.' It goes without saying that none of the designs representing this third group found their way on to the 1951 'stock list' of items chosen by the CoID for display at the South Bank Festival site.

Once again, it seems, the centrist mood of the Labour Party had filtered its way through the CoID to affect design for the Festival. It was, after all, the government who had the final say as to what items were included in the Festival exhibitions and, as had been the case in 1851, the Festival of Britain was intended to show off British manufacturing strengths, never to rock the boat. It had been controversial from the start – the Tories had been very much against such an extravagant showcase – so the Festival's organizers and designers must have been restricted from making the show too avant garde. In any case it had always been the intention that the Festival should be genuinely populist. Given the personalities of the politicians involved in the Festival, (as Festival spokesman in the House of Commons, Herbert Morrison was its chief protagonist), it is hardly surprising that the event represented a rather middle-of-the-road celebration of British achievement.

Through Utility (both during and after the war) and through Britain Can Make It and the Festival of Britain it has been possible to assess the influence of the ideology behind state-backed design. But this is only one side of the picture. Government commitment to design as a means of social and economic amelioration would mean nothing unless the Board of Trade could harness the interest and experience of the trade itself. To assess the extent to which manufacturers were prepared to act in concert with the CoID and other government bodies, we must examine the furniture trade itself. This, together with an analysis of public response to the Utility Scheme and to post-war design, forms the second part of this book.

PART II

Figure 6.1

CHAPTER 6

Utility and the Furniture Trade:
A 'Totalitarian Plot'

'This is the beginning of a "closed shop" in art.'
The Cabinet Maker, 7 December 1946

The extreme suspicion with which the furniture trade viewed government intervention into design was evident almost as soon as control and rationing were announced. As early as February 1940 an editorial in *The Cabinet Maker* (CM) stated that there were

> grounds for the grave suspicion that some policy of control, and a very great deal of its detail, are dictated and arranged by people who are the open advocates of a system of society different from that under which we are accustomed to live. These folk are making the most of the opportunity which present circumstances give to them, and a steady flow of official speeches and announcements show how their ideas have been woven into the present national habits.

Presuming that the CM voiced majority opinion within the furniture trade, its members clearly felt that they and the British Isles at large, were about to fall prey to a particularly virulent strain of that nastiest of diseases, socialism. This fear, evidently made worse by the feeling that the scourge had crept in through the back door, was to continue unabated until the Labour Party's defeat in 1951.

It is important to note both the tenor and the timing of the trade's initial dissension. Although its loathing of government intervention into trade escalated once the Utility Scheme came into operation, it was not always control per se that caused the ill will. Underlying the furniture trade's antipathy was its sense that the traditional values which were integral to the structure of the industry itself were threatened by an alien political system. This fear needs looking into in greater detail before an assessment can be made of the more specific criticisms levelled by the trade at utility furniture. In view of its ideological resistance to the state control of industry it is entirely to the furniture trade's credit that it resolved to act in compliance with the Board of Trade's dictates, not that it had a great deal of choice. Its reasons for doing so were set out somewhat melodramatically in the CM editorial of March 1941: 'We have to fight total war to avoid enslavement and utter ruin, and the furniture trade is a small thing compared with that. If, therefore, this production policy is essential we must swallow it, with a wry grimace maybe, but with full accord and readiness to help.' This was before the full enormity of government control had hit. On the announcement of the Utility Scheme for furniture, the CM was quick to condemn the programme as being 'thoroughly bad'. By the next issue, however, it appears to have decided that to rail against the scheme would be unpatriotic and therefore negate the very moral code that it was itself fighting to maintain.

> When the gallant defenders of Stalingrad are calling for munitions which could be made in our factories ... can we honestly or patriotically protest because the government have temporarily placed a ban on trade activities ... The point has been reached when the furniture trade must submit to ruthless restrictions which, we are convinced, it will accept in a truly patriotic spirit recognizing that today's thunderstorm brings forth tomorrow's flowers – and they will be flowers of a beauty hitherto unknown – we shall grumble, we shouldn't be British if we didn't, but we shall accept the inevitable.

The fierce patriotism that grudgingly won the trade over to the government's side provides a clue as to its abhorrence of control.

In essence, the furniture trade's sentiment, according to the CM, was that state intervention was profoundly undemocratic and, axiomatically, unBritish. Furthermore, while this situation could be justified in war, it was felt to be profoundly sinister after the cessation of hostilities. By 1945 the CM was voicing the opinion that 'Britishness' and British values had now won two world wars, but that this spirit was now in greater jeopardy than ever before. Continuing controls meant the continuing erosion of the great tradition of Freedom, which would be 'repugnant to the deepest instincts of Britishers throughout the Commonwealth'. In June 1945 a CM editorial responded to altered conditions:

> In facing the facts of to-day, in immediately tackling the problems which call for solution, we can still be clear as to the course which we desire to follow and the goal that we desire to reach. That goal is Freedom. Freedom from all controls not essential for the prosecution of the war or the transition of war to peace; freedom to adven-

ture our resources, our skill and our initiative as free men, and not as obedient myrmidons of a totalitarian state.

The trade did not simply fear for itself, however. Britain Can Make It ('totalitarian art' par excellence) provided the CM with an opportunity to point out that efforts to coerce the public were also becoming endemic: 'Behind and above it all [that is, 'Britain Can Make It'] is a well-planned attempt to secure control of public taste, and great significance must attach to the hatching of such a plot within the hallowed portals of the Victoria and Albert.' That the fears of the furniture trade over the brainwashing of the general public were to prove completely unfounded will form the subject of the next chapter. What is significant here is that the trade believed that 'consumer control' was rife. The CM was even convinced that the 'CC' of the 'CC41' utility mark stood for 'consumer control'; its actual meaning was 'civilian clothing'. The deep mistrust with which the trade viewed the Labour Party does not provide the full story, however. Specific criticisms of utility emerged which cannot be attributed simply to the clash with socialism.

In the face of the creeping threat of socialism, the British furniture trade of the 1940s was able to present a remarkably united front. But there were internal squabbles. Differences came to light particularly once the Utility Scheme was imposed since this brought with it a super-structural organization which meant that previously disparate branches of the industry were now all too well aware of what others were doing. Zoning, for example, heightened tensions and was a much criticized system of rationalization. Standardized design (which was to facilitate production by any firm no matter what its previous manufacturing history), was disliked by manufacturers in certain areas who wanted jealously to guard their own specialist skills.

Former High Wycombe trade member Maurice Clarke says that, belonging to the traditional centre of chair-making, Wycombe manufacturers were considerably put out about the fact that, for example, 'lots of people were designated to make chairs in the North, and they weren't very experienced'. Also, 'If you got an inspector from Wycombe you were all right but if you got one from one of the other areas, they'd make you do things that were wrong just because they didn't know.'

In High Wycombe at least, the feeling seems to have been that utility ran the risk of bringing the trade into disrepute because of poor standards reached by firms unused to furniture manufacture. In fact, specifications and quality control were so rigorous and the penalties for failing to comply with them so draconian[1] that to manufacture furniture that was not up to scratch would have required enormous ingenuity. Even if zoning had had no worrying political ramifications, this was an aspect of control that was hard to bear since it went right against the spirit of fierce independence which the trade held so dear.

An even greater source of frustration, particularly to the quality furniture makers, was the total lack of scope for any creativity. Even when, in 1948, 'Freedom of Design' allowed manufacturers to produce their own designs within Board of Trade-specified dimensions, little could be done to stray from the specifications to which the trade had by this time been working for six years and resentment understandably mounted. David Joel's wry comments on this matter must be typical of the opinion of the furniture trade; 'Latterly it was possible, after endless visits and correspondence to obtain a licence to make a small coffee table, provided the timber content did not exceed some minute fraction of a cubic foot' (Joel 1953, p.134).

The next blow was the Prices of Goods Act. To the injury of no longer being free to fix its own profit margins, was added the insulting implication that the public was being protected from a profiteering trade. Retailers too appeared to want to re-establish relations with their pre-war suppliers, as was mentioned particularly in the Reconversion of Civil Industry meetings. It is interesting that despite the Utility Scheme's by-passing of the old established network of distribution between manufacturer and retailer, the furniture trade repeatedly voiced its concern as to the plight of that network. One could be cynical and attribute this to the trade's wish to protect its own commercial outlets for the post-war period. In fact, one of the trade's chief worries was for the retailer: as had been recognized on the beginning of the Utility Scheme, it would be a long time before any of the furniture was actually in the shops. And when it did come on the market, would anyone want to buy it? According to Maurice Clarke, on its first appearance Utility was generally thought to be 'a bit too modernistic for the average'. Clarke believed that the Utility Furniture Advisory Committee had been taken over by designers (or worse still – although actually there were none on the committee – that evil beast, the architect). Having little idea of what was going on at grass roots level, nor any understanding as to why the public should prefer traditional styles, the UFAC wanted to assert their own ideas as to what constituted good design. 'You see,' said Clarke,

> between the wars there was this Paris exhibition and that was supposed to be the, *the* advanced way of going on and all the rest of it.

> The panel was full of the sort of people who began flashing about before the war. Elizabeth Denby – Mr Barnes said of Elizabeth Denby – 'she's the sort of person who puts a yellow tablecloth on and that's the scheme' you see, anybody like that tried to get on . . . .[2]

> Gordon Russell, you see, was known to a certain type of the public, as being a rather fine designer; industrial designer and all the rest of it. But, you see, to the trade he was rather airy fairy. But he was a very nice man. Mr Barnes always said he liked him as a man but not as a designer.

Worse than this, the trade linked modernism with an erosion of craftsmanship. Maurice Clarke still feels vehemently that the Utility Scheme was responsible for a lot of damage in this direction.

> That's one of the problems there was with Utility. Everyone had to make the same thing which meant you didn't need an apprentice because you'd got nothing to teach him on. The last few years, the last ten or twenty years we've felt the effects of the Utility programme; that did a dickens of a lot of harm, you see. I said it would at the time. I said all this business will mean that we have no craftsmen. But they just said well we can't help that and brushed it on one side.

> You see there's another thing with all these committees, they had to design stuff which could be made all over the country, so you were down to the lowest sort of form. It had to be very very plain and absolutely cut right down to the bone. And architects started coming in and saying that there shouldn't be any carving: 'carving is a silly thing, cut it out'.[3]

Strongly felt though they were, none of these criticisms was simply the product of ideological resistance to the Board of Trade's organization of the furniture industry; each made a valid point of its own. Equally, no criticism was made of the standards of design. Although it disliked the style of utility furniture, the trade had the good grace to concede that the quality of design and of construction were high. A 'letter' written to the editor of CM on the first showing of the furniture to the trade makes it obvious that despite other reservations, the trade believed firmly in giving credit where it was due. The last word on the trade's attitude should go to 'John Brown of Anytown' writing in October 1942 on 'Utility Furniture. How it strikes me':

Since you ask me, Mr Editor, I'll tell you what I think of the utility furniture you let me see the other day. It certainly is remarkable stuff, but of course the public won't like it and it's no good pretending they will. I'm one of them and I know what I like and what my neighbours and my Cousin Billy of London Town like.

Of course we can take it – we shall have to – although I wish I knew what the price was, and maybe helped out with bits and pieces we can gather together from the good old days, and in our snug rooms it won't seem too bad.

I don't like being too high falutin, but if you know what I mean there is a melancholy strain in the great British public, and although Mr Gloag (after all Mr Gloag is a Scot, so maybe takes a more logical view of things) don't like that sentimental strain, we can't help a bit of addiction to what we think is smart and/or old fashioned.

From what you say sir, this utility furniture is actually a bit more like what our ancestors really had in periods of great craftsmanship and good taste than what we buy, or did buy up until a year or two ago, in this age.

And I will say this Mr Editor, the stuff looks good. I'll say that of all of it, and what's more, although I'm no expert, far from it, on furniture, it *is good* – anyone can see that. But why did Mr Dalton appoint a *committee* to design it. Why, I could have designed it myself: in fact there is no design in it. Nothing to give it an 'Olde Worlde' touch. No twists, no applied decoration. Well now I wonder if that's why I can tell, even though I'm no expert, as I said, that it *is* good and it *looks* good . . .

How easily the drawers and cupboards in the bedroom stuff moved! A real treat. Most of mine (although, if you'll pardon me, I think the ones I've got are much posher) won't work after a few year's wear. I've got a fancy that these would though . . . .

How will the prices look. The workmanship's all right, and I suppose the appearance is too, but you know best about that. Price is the thing though. Still, as my Cousin Billy would say (only he's a poet and I'm not):

'This stuff is here for your correction,
although it fails to stir affection.'

Good, solid and sensible that's just what the public doesn't like – except in the kitchen, when I find that Mrs Brown (and Cousin Billy's Mrs too) become more functional than H G Wells.

Was John Brown's attitude reflective of the feeling of the rest of the country? An analysis of public response to the Utility Scheme as a whole, to utility furniture more specifically, and to post-war design in general may provide the answer.

NOTES

1   *The Cabinet Maker*, 12 September 1942 records that

> A fine of £500 each – the maximum pecuniary penalty – or failing payment in a month, three months' imprisonment, was at Paisley Sheriff Court on Monday, imposed by Sheriff Hamilton on Andrew Davidson and John McIlwaine, managing director and director respectively of William Simons and Co. Ltd, Renfrew, who pleaded guilty on indictment, of using timber and plywood contrary to the Control of Timber Orders made under the Defence (General) Regulations.

2   Elizabeth Denby was a member of the Utility Furniture Advisory Committee. Mr Barnes was a designer for Goodearls of High Wycombe.

3   A letter written by Maurice Clarke to the Board of Trade, 18 August 1949, makes very much the same point about the furniture shown at Britain Can Make It:

> In the Britain Can Make It exhibition the furniture on show was

almost exclusively of the modern type . . . I consider that the Board of Trade have been very badly advised with regard to the type of furniture that should be shown at such exhibitions. We find that they are advised by architects and the more 'arty-crafty' designer. The architect always favours plain stuff, and you will find that their designs in the main, are copies at least, or are based on the continental, and this type of furniture can probably be best obtained from the continental countries. Official encouragement should be given in some way or another to maintaining a certain amount of carved work in this country . . . we are losing our skill; this is to be deplored.

CHAPTER 7

Utility and the Public: a Misunderstanding

'I liked the utility furniture least of all. It looked too
precarious and weak. I don't care much for modern
furniture.' (Clerk's wife, 49)

'I like that modern stuff . . . Do you? – It *is* very nice – it's
the lines of it I like.' (35-year-old couple, artisan)
Comments recorded by Mass Observation on furniture
exhibits shown at 'Britain Can Make It'

In its annual report for the year 1946–47 the CoID was able to note 'a
quickening of interest' in design matters among traders, manufacturers
and also the general public. This is attributed to the impact made by
'Britain Can Make It':

> while a well-staged exhibition of consumer goods, coming after
> seven years of war, would have evoked considerable interest in any
> circumstances, we are satisfied that a good deal of interest was
> aroused in the minds of visitors by the actual design of the goods
> shown and the idea of design itself. 'We think BCMI was a consider-
> able step forward in the process, and we well know that it will be a
> long one, of arousing a more discriminating attitude towards design
> among the public generally.'

Similarly, the following year the report could comment on the fact that
increasing calls were being made on its library and publication facilities,
and that enquiries from both the public as well as the private sector were
pouring in. The enthusiasm with which the Board of Trade approached the
task of reconstruction via exhibition does seem to have gone some way
towards affecting an increased consideration of the benefits of good design
for everyday life. The post-war mood of optimism which was at once the
reason for and the result of the Labour Party's astounding victory in 1945[1]
had created an environment in which everyone from the politician to the
man in the street became a vociferous propagandist for the visionary
Utopia. Everyone had their own opinion as to how the new Britain should
be built and to some extent this appears to have galvanized an interest in
the concept of design for the future as set in motion by the government.
'Planning' now entered public parlance. In January 1945 Misha Black
could write in the vehemently populist *Picture Post* that the need to plan
town and country developments was gaining recognition. Significantly, he

could also wonder: 'Are we to be content with patterns which were in the shops in 1939, or is it possible to improve the interiors of our homes as radically as we want to improve our towns and houses?' Before the war sentiments like this had been common, having been expressed by the CAI and DIA among other institutions. However, for a designer to address an audience in so direct a manner was a radical and, it seems, welcome departure.

Increased awareness of design in the abstract is one thing, the central question here, however, is whether, as Gordon Russell and others believed, the effects of utility and systematized government-backed intervention in design had actually altered taste. What of the new design itself? What sort of public reaction did it meet?

More to the point, how does one arrive, more than 40 years on, at public response to the products which began to appear on the market in post-war Britain? Fortunately a combination of the Attlee administration's anxiety to establish the mood of its citizens together with the unstinting efforts of Mass Observation (MO) go some way towards providing answers to these questions.

In their inimitable style, MO workers were on hand at BCMI to interview people as they journeyed around the exhibition. While the methods of data collection employed by MO were not always particularly sophisticated (eavesdropping constituting at least part of the system), reports are invaluable as they recorded spontaneous public reaction.

As the quotations at the start of this chapter indicate, attitudes towards the products on display at BCMI varied enormously. On the whole, however, opinion came down heavily against 'the modern'. Many felt that new design was not felt to be homely: 'I don't like the ultra-modern designs – I like what's cosy and neat' (housewife married to an engineer). This was especially evident in the case of the steel furniture (see, for example, Figure 7.1) which was felt to be far too functional:

> I don't like that steel furniture. I wouldn't buy it. It's not at all snug or cosy. It looks too much like an aircraft factory. (26-year-old artisan)
> Looks like cold steel does. (26-year-old-woman, artisan)
> I do not like that steel stuff. I wouldn't have known that was a sideboard – looks more like a 'fridge to me. It's a good job it's labelled. (24-year-old artisan)

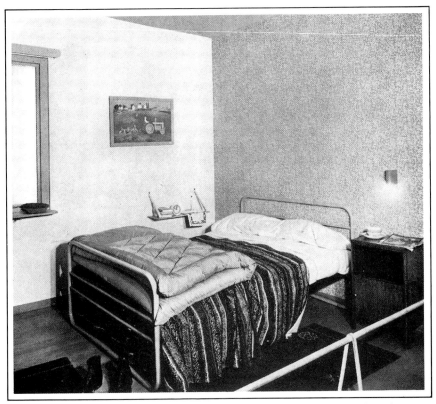

Figure 7.1   Steel bed, an exhibit at 'Britain Can Make It'

Despite the example set by the BCMI 'Furnished Rooms' section, it seems that home-making for the larger part of the British public was still deeply rooted in the emotional comfort afforded by more traditional styles. Both 'cosy' and 'comfortable' appear frequently in the quoted reasons for liking or disliking an exhibit. Interesting too is the attitude of a '36-year-old artisan' who, commenting on a winged chair, provided one of the few favourable responses to the furniture but he added, 'although it's modern it looks like the real antique thing.' He went on, 'I do not like this modern stuff, it's alright for half an hour, but after that I'd leave home.'

The CoID's aim to persuade the public that good simple design could be as homely as that of the pre-war era was clearly not having the desired effect. Nearly all the positive remarks recorded by MO are related to the kitchen. For example: ' "I'm impressed with some of the advancements in the kitchens that I hadn't visualized, all spotless and modern" (electrician)'. Indeed the kitchen was just beginning to acquire something of the glamorous efficiency of its American counterpart. It can be argued that kitchens, and perhaps bathrooms, were the first domestic spaces to be modernized. However, this had very little to do with professional attempts to lick design into shape and much more to do with attitudes towards cleanliness, hygiene and the changing role and status of women. Easy-to-clean modern fittings and labour-saving gadgets were welcomed. Elsewhere in the house, people were less willing to relinquish their traditional concept of 'home'. There also seemed to remain, despite the valiant efforts of the CoID, a strong association between traditional style and quality; an artisan who did not like modern furniture said, '-3ply, 5-ply, that's what it amounts to'. An appendix to MO's BCMI report provides the findings of an enquiry specifically organized to compare utility furniture with that shown in other areas of the exhibition. It reaches the sorry conclusion that:

> People were just not interested in utility furniture; few looked at this part of section 19, and fewer still commented favourably on it. Utility seems to have acquired a reputation for flimsiness and poor quality, and most of the comments emphasize this.
> 'I wouldn't have anything like it in my home. It's a damn shame that these young people just setting up home have to deal with this sort of furniture because within a few years it won't be worth a farthing.' (upper working class man of 40)

It may simply be that modern furniture had not yet had time to prove its durability. But the level of reaction suggests deep and emotional associations between quality and tradition. It is ironic that utility furniture, into which an enormous amount of time, care and attention had been poured in an effort to guarantee high standards, was compared unfavourably with furniture of the pre-war period which in fact might well have been 'knocked together' only a few months earlier. When this attitude finally began to crumble, it was not necessarily as a result of CoID initiatives, nor indeed of the experience of Utility.

In spring 1945 the government's social survey body, in conjunction with the CoID, was commissioned to conduct an enquiry for the Board of Trade into the popularity of utility furniture. Taking a random sample of housewives and a more specific sample of women whose names and addresses were available through the lists of those holding dockets enabling them to buy the furniture, it asked interviewees to indicate satisfaction with the quality, design and style of the furniture that they had seen in the shops or actually owned. On the whole findings were favourable: over half of those questioned responded positively when asked how much they liked their furniture.[2]

However, this result was by no means the full story. Particularly keen to assess current popular taste in furniture, the CoID organized a second section to the investigation. In this, interviewees were asked to choose their favourite piece from a number of photographs of bedroom furniture.[3] The first photograph, to use the report's terminology, depicted 'plain and fairly modern furniture', the second 'more old fashioned' furniture and the third and fourth both 'extremely modern' styles. Of the random sample, 45 per cent picked the furniture in photograph 2 as their first choice, against 27 per cent preferring that in photograph 1 to all of the others.[4] Among the utility owners, however, equal numbers (36 per cent) gave photograph 1 or 2 as their first choice.

It may seem harsh to undermine this small and somewhat rare triumph for the Gordon Russell school of thought, but one should note the way in which these percentages were broken down into age groups. Of those choosing the furniture shown in the first picture, 39 per cent were under 34 years old (24 per cent were older). The items in the second photograph were the first choice of 30 per cent of the under-34 age group and 49 per cent of the older group. It is likely then that the relative popularity of utility furniture among its owners had as much to do with age as with a re-education of taste.

It may be that the MO survey of BCMI did not reflect fairly the extent to which the utility Scheme and the CoID influenced public taste. Coming so soon after the end of the war, the exhibition was held at an awkward time. Utility had, as intended become synonymous in the public mind with a kind of straightforward modernity. But its simplicity of form was associated with shortages of materials and thus structural instability, as the remarks quoted earlier made clear. Since the public was well aware in 1946 that rationing was set to continue indefinitely, the timing of BCMI was in some ways hardly propitious, and in all likelihood (although intended to do just the opposite) it off-set the Board of Trade's enthusiastic proclamations about the potential of modern design for building the new Britain.[5]

In the autumn of 1950 the Board of Trade commissioned an enquiry – 'Utility and the Public' – to establish the reaction of the general public to the Utility Scheme as the basis for assessing whether or not it should continue. Between 12 September and 3 October 1950, interviewees were asked about their attitude towards government involvement in production for the civilian market, towards price and quality control and about the level of knowledge of the scheme. Of the 57 per cent in favour of a system which safeguarded the quality of consumer goods, only 13 per cent thought that the government should be directly responsible for this, 20 per cent thinking that the government should act merely to persuade manufacturers to safeguard quality. When it came to the question of government involvement as a means of controlling price, however, there was rather more interest. Forty-nine per cent were in favour of a greater standardization of styles if this would bring a reduction in cost. The report concluded that:

> People are moderately concerned about quality being controlled. There is little opposition to the idea but one person in four expresses no opinion. On the other hand, there is widespread feeling amongst all sections of the population in favour of fixing the price of some goods that may not be exceeded.

Clearly the most important aspect of the CoID's message had not penetrated very deeply. This failing was further borne out by the fact that the report's survey of first associations with the scheme found price to be the consideration that had made the most impact and the quality of goods mentioned had come second. In the end the survey was forced to conclude that:

> Initiated to some extent as a means of safeguarding quality, during a time of severe shortage and when 'austerity' was the rule in most things, the scheme might have been regarded as a blessing in times of need or as a makeshift method of getting over war-time difficulties by providing people with something which was at any rate 'better than nothing'.

However, it continued:

> Subsequent experience of utility goods, when the conditions of shortage have been altered and when it is obvious that utility prices are far more within the means of the majority of people than the prices of most non-utility goods, might well result in inclining people towards a favourable view of utility, but the fact that the range

of styles was, until fairly recently, limited in comparison with the range of styles in non-utility goods might well have had the opposite effect.

The fact that quality and simplicity of design had not won the hearts of the general public is also indicated by the fact that of the 60 per cent in favour of continuing the scheme as a means of price control, only a small number were in favour of this if it involved specified design (6 per cent in the case of furniture design and 21 per cent in the case of clothing; this larger figure presumably due to the fact that clothes had never been subject to rigorous government specification in any case).

It is hardly surprising in the light of these results that the Utility Scheme was abandoned the following year, 1951, particularly since this was also the year in which Attlee's administration was defeated by the Conservatives. By this time the socialist/CoID alliance had at least succeeded in fostering a new design consciousness among the general public. As has been said, more and more people had become aware of design not just as a remote professional practice but as something which had a valid part to play in their daily lives. There is much less evidence, however, as to how general public taste had been reformed either by the example of utility or by government-backed intervention through the CoID. Indeed, those changes in taste which did take place could not be conclusively attributed to either of these.

To assess how the passage of time affected people's attitudes, it is necessary to look at a couple of later exhibitions and surveys.

Register Your Choice was organized by the Design and Industries Association (DIA), and staged at Charing Cross in 1953. Once again Mass Observation was on the scene to interview visitors as they emerged from the displays and to write down comments overheard inside. The exhibition consisted of two dining rooms, and the public were asked to vote according to which one they preferred. Room L (Figure 7.2) was furnished with homely, comfortable, dark, old-fashioned furniture and fittings, typical of the inter-war period. Room R (Figure 7.3) was set out with furniture of the sort of softened modernity that had been the key-note at BCMI. Voting resulted in triumph for the new, Room R receiving 18,188 votes against Room L's 12,146. Mass Observation corroborated this win: 65 per cent of interviewees preferred Room R. However, recorded comments indicate that whereas Room R represented the best of contem-

Figure 7.2   Room L, 'Register Your Choice'

Figure 7.3   Room R, 'Register Your Choice'

porary design, Room L was an example of the worst of its type. 'The left hand room (supposedly conventional) has been quite deliberately played down and the choice is therefore *grossly* unfair. A conventional furnished room chosen with good taste would bear some comparison with Room R and a fair choice be given.' Furthermore, as one of the more sympathetic comments pointed out, 'I do not think that the room L has been decorated in fairness to those who prefer the homely and comfortable. For example, such people I consider would certainly choose their carpet to match the furniture.'

The public was not, it seemed about to toe the CoID line. Where Room R was commented upon favourably it was always with the caveat that it could have been made much more 'homely' and 'comfortable':

> The chairs in R while being comfortable and attractive looking, don't keep out draughts and one or two of them would be enough, with something more comfortable. I think R will date awfully quickly, and it is a bit precious but, of course, on the whole it's first class. I think L has been made worse than the average room of its kind.

Similarly, someone else wrote:

> Room R is very attractive in every way but from a comfort point of view under actual living conditions in winter, inadequate heating would be apparent. The modern furniture is excellent providing that the standard of living is able to include some form of central heating.

Nevertheless, as this last comment indicates, whether or not contemporary design was liked, there was a recognition of its quality in terms of a new clarity, simplicity and airiness. Once again though, any claims for the success of government-backed intervention and its role in redefining taste must take into account the fact that the modern room was predominantly chosen by under-35-year-olds. Their choice may well have represented a deliberate desire to create an environment distinct from that of their parents' and typified by Room L.[6]

By 1957 the DIA obviously felt that the public had made some progress, and rather than present viewers with a straightforward choice between 'good' and 'bad' design, it made the test slightly trickier. At Make or Mar?, again held at Charing Cross, they exhibited two contemporary rooms, the right-hand one badly designed, the left-hand one restful and harmonious. The DIA described it as a 'subtle essay in "do's and don'ts" ' (Figure 7.4).

Above. The 'Make' room.
Below. The 'Mar' room.

Figure 7.4   The two rooms at 'Make or Mar'?

The long-suffering public responded to this latest quizzing of its taste in understandably weary tones: 'I would probably shoot myself in either room, but would definitely prefer to do it in the left-hand room.'

What part was played by retailers in the process of changing public taste during this period is not easy to decide. The high street multiples, selling, it was presumed, to the working class, were often blamed by the design reformers for the public's refusal to refurnish in a contemporary style. This view was based on the rather patronizing concept of a proletariat who only had to be shown what to do for them to do it but who, for the meantime, continued to make mistakes because they were being set no better example. Gordon Russell summed up the design reformer's lament when he described the 'flashy and meretricious goods' which gave 'an impression of luxury and costliness to the ignorant when seen from the pavement and skilfully lighted' (Russell 1953, p.59).

In an essay on the retailer as taste-maker in *Did Britain Make It?*, Penny Sparke suggests that the role of the retailer provides the missing link in the reform/popular consumption polemic. Very much a chicken and egg situation, it is now very difficult to assess whether the public got the furniture that it wanted or whether it simply got what it was given. The CoID view was that blame lay squarely at the feet of the multiple retailer because, at least until the consumer spending boom of the second half of the 1950s, many of these shops relied heavily upon and consequently encouraged, hire purchase. This, it was argued, produced a situation in which retailers could not afford to take financial risks and therefore refused to buy in more innovatory designs. The end result of this was that an overblown ornamental style was relied upon instead to produce novelty and saleability as it had a capacity for endless variation.

Perhaps hire purchase did restrict the pace at which new designs were introduced into the high street shops, but it cannot be said to have greatly impeded reform of public taste since there was no reason why retailers should not have sold cheaper makes of 'contemporary' furniture on hire purchase.

The speed of change in patterns of domestic consumption was influenced much more by a number of socio-economic factors. In its 1990 exhibition, Putting On The Style – Setting Up Home In The 1950s, the Geffrye Museum chose to examine just this theme. The exhibition's room sets and displays were based on the experiences of people who had married and bought furniture for their homes. Interviews revealed a much more flexible attitude towards interior decoration and furniture than the CoID would ever have accorded the general public at the time. Nevertheless, as the exhibition catalogue makes clear, many people were very conscious of the prevailing taste of their peer group when choosing furniture. It was all very well for Gordon Russell to tell you what to put in your home but it was not Gordon Russell who was going to call round or be entertained in your front room. To suggest that social pressure was an overwhelming factor in choice of furniture is to make the same mistake that the design reformers made of seeing the working class as a monolithic mass; but contemporary reports do indicate that for most people a 'what will the neighbours think?' concern had at least some influence upon their purchases. A 23-year-old shorthand typist interviewed at Register Your Choice made the point perfectly:

> R is ideal – need I say more. Wonderful warm tones of colour are picked up all around the room. But I would never live in it. For one thing my family would have a fit, they'd think I'd gone quite mad and all arty. You see I'd have to be a different person, I'd have to read the best books and listen to the third programme, don't you agree?

Perhaps it was too much to expect that sweeping changes in popular aesthetic choices could have been made during the period between 1943 when the first utility furniture became available and the Festival of Britain in 1951. Eight years is a very short time in which to clear away emotionally entrenched tastes. This is not to say that the experience of utility was wasted, however. Even before 1951, all the signs were that the sort of quasi-modernism initiated, and to some degree exemplified, by the scheme was to play a major role in the rebuilding of Britain. The atrocious planning which ensued in the 1960s is another story; in 1951 there was great optimism and belief in the utility idiom's potential for renewal. In the concluding chapter we review the mainpoints covered earlier to understand how a programme which started on such an ideological high note should fail, in its own terms, to make the desired impact on either the general public or the furniture trade.

NOTES

1 Labour won 393 seats against 210 to the Conservatives and allies and 12 to the Liberals.

2   *Appeal of utility furniture design*

	%		%
Likes it.	51	Dislikes it	16
Likes it with reservations.	9	No definite judgement	16
Likes certain specifications but not others	8		

3   Unfortunately these photographs were missing from the Board of Trade file.

4   *Frequency of preference of the four photographs*

	Random sample %	Utility furniture sample %
1	27	36
2	45	36
3	13	13
4	12	10
Didn't like any	1	1
Couldn't decide	2	4

5   The exhibition was dubbed 'Britain Can't Have It' by a sceptical press and public.

6   Denis Chapman's survey, 'The Home and Social Status, 1955' provides accounts given by sales staff of the dissension between parents and children when shopping for furniture.

> Occasionally the couples' parents accompany them. The sales-men were unanimous that when this happened a great deal of difficulty arose. They considered that it was unusual for parents and children to agree and, to some extent, it was a revolt against the furniture with which they had been brought up.

CONCLUSION

'I think in retrospect, that we made some impact on the trade, although much of that advantage has been frittered away.'

Gordon Russell, interviewed in September 1974

Gordon Russell's thoughts in 1974 contrast poignantly with the enthusiastic urgency of his early mission. It also begs an answer to the question, what went wrong? It has been the thesis of this book that as a result of the particular political conditions of the 1940s design increasingly came under the aegis of the state. Nowhere was this more apparent than in the manufacture of utility furniture which was subject to the minutiae of Board of Trade specifications. To understand the design of this furniture, I have argued that it is necessary to look at the particular beliefs of those involved in its production. Following this line of argument, it seems likely that an explanation for the outcome of government intervention would be found in Board of Trade ideology.

Since utility furniture was produced by a team of design-conscious men and women working under the socialist directorship of the Board of Trade, the historical nature of the alliance between the socialists and aesthetic reformers is particularly important. By unravelling the several strands that made up the fabric of this collaboration, it should be possible to determine whether there were any factors intrinsic to the partnership which predicated the influence that utility was to have.

Clement Attlee is recorded as having said that far from being merely a political creed or an economic system, socialism is 'a philosophy of society'. There have been a number of occasions in British history when the warp of politics has been interwoven with the weft of an aesthetic vision for the future.

One such moment was provided by the Arts and Crafts movement of the late nineteenth century. Arts and Crafts aesthetics centred around a return to a pre-industrial set of values and way of life and, while the movement did not define itself first and foremost in terms of a political creed, its vision did have particular implications for social amelioration. It was the belief of both John Ruskin and William Morris that the evils of industrial production should be rejected in favour of a return to a medieval system of craft-based manufacture.

Correlli Barnett, among others, has argued that the Arts and Crafts hatred of industrial society was part of a strain in British culture, deeply mistrustful of industrialization, that can be traced back to early nineteenth-century romanticist sanctuary from modern life in 'the beautiful other worlds of the imagination' (Barnett, 1986, p.14). Indeed Britain took the Arts and Crafts style and worked it into a humanistic but deeply paternalistic view of both aesthetic and social amelioration.

Given the heady mix of romanticism and medievalism that comprised the Ruskin–Morris utopian construct, one begins to wonder whether the socialist/aesthetic alliance was at all aware of the realities of twentieth-century life. It is one of the paradoxes of British design history, however, that this conservative ideology actually slotted very neatly alongside a view of the human condition and its amelioration that was entirely the product of modern life.

Again the result of a cross-pollination of political and aesthetic ideas, the second ideological thread had its roots in European modernism. Continental modernists had a deterministic vision of social amelioration through an improvement of everyone's surroundings. Their doctrine had been an important element of the rhetoric of avant garde radicalism. In crossing the channel European modernism had to be modified so as not to offend British sensibilities, and it is therefore extremely difficult to trace a direct correlation between modernism and socialism in Britain; it was a watered down version of the *spirit*, but not the style, of modernism that was to form the second strand of the alliance between the socialists and the aesthetic reformers.

The awakening from 'splendid isolation' that was represented by the appropriation of modernist ideology was also the cause of a growing recognition that on the Continent design was increasingly being used as a means of dealing with industrialized life. Far from the rejection of mass production that lay at the heart of the romanticist/Ruskinian vision of design, the Europeans, it seemed, had actually formulated a principle for the improvement of industrial manufacture. Had this not had implications for foreign economic competition, it is likely that the insular British would have remained untroubled by the aesthetic debates taking place in Europe.

The threat of foreign superiority – the Germans in particular could be seen to be making decisive strides in this direction – was, however, enough to activate an increasingly pragmatic approach to industrial manufacture. Furthermore, in the early years of this century, as industrialization appeared set to stay, socialists began to argue that its proceeds could at least be used in an egalitarian sharing of wealth. That these socialists could not be accused of that dangerous practice of internationalism was itself due to Britain's own industrial history and its Empire. Indeed, the practical approach to manufacture that formed the third strand of the socialist/aesthetic experience had been born at a time when imperialism was at its height.

It is another example of the complexity of the times that a vision for social reform through industrial wealth was accommodated alongside the romanticist rejection of mass production as the ultimate evil. Despite this clash of interests, the desire to harness good design to the products of industry as a means of boosting economic growth had been the raison d'être for the Great Exhibition of 1851, and, in the twentieth century, it had been sufficiently strong a force to establish the Design and Industries Association in 1914. Ingrained, at least as an element of the ideology of the liberal left, this practical approach to design and industry was to reach its apotheosis in the post-war design debates of the 1940s.

The economic conditions of the Second World War strengthened the role of pragmatism in the socialist/aesthetic alliance. Design, rather than being merely an economic booster, became an economic necessity. Under the socialist leadership of the Board of Trade good design became an axiom of the need to balance continued manufacturing for the civilian market with the efficient use of drastically restricted resources.

The careful consideration of design also became part of the Board of Trade's contribution to maintaining Home Front morale by providing quality goods for those most in need. Thus the guaranteed quality that utility production ensured became a very significant element of war socialism.

Another key characteristic of socialist ideology of the 1941–45 period was its tendency towards collectivism which became more pronounced as the war progressed and as government responsibility for the wellbeing of its citizens became the central tenet of the vision of a welfare state. Reconstruction assured design a dynamic role in the creation of a better

Britain. And, since the quasi-modernist vision of the political/aesthetic alliance tended to justify the raising of living conditions by a design-based improvement of the physical objects of human surroundings, it seemed that the romanticist, conservative strand in the partnership had finally been overcome.

Certainly, if *The Cabinet Maker* were to be believed, the new dynamism of socialism represented an unstoppable force set to undermine the way of life and set of values dear to every true 'Britisher'. That *The Cabinet Maker* should take this stance in fact says much more about the political affiliations of the furniture trade than it does about the radicalism of the British left. The trade's great fear was that, in imposing a brash new style of design, the 'totalitarian' state would erode both trade independence and craftsmanship. The fear that skills would be lost was understandable, but entirely unjustified. The trade's assumptions about the nature of socialism were wrong, but its opinion that at best the public would only put up with utility furniture in the short term and because it had to was quite right. And, ironically, public reception of the designs produced under Board of Trade initiative was as much a response to the conservatism of the socialists as it was to the imposition of a 'modern' aesthetic.

Despite the vigorous promotion of design as an essential for the raising of living standards, the furniture shown at Britain Can Make It manifested a traditionalism which suggested that the romanticism of the Arts and Crafts thread in the socialists' creed was very much alive and well. Clearly the new concept of design as a strategy for reconstruction had not been translated into any radical departure in style. A possible explanation for this is the enduring conservatism of the Labour Party at this time. Indeed the very concept of a reform of public taste, central to the socialist/ aesthetic debate and the ultimate goal of the utility furniture programme, was the result of a rather hidebound, paternalistic attitude towards society.

It was an attitude which failed to understand, or rather, chose to ignore, a set of values and way of life. There is no question that the whole drive for reform and its attendant prescription of design aesthetics was aimed primarily at the working class. The 'we know what is best for you' attitude paid no regard to issues of cultural autonomy. In his seminal work *The Uses of Literacy*, Richard Hoggart said of working class culture of the 1950s that at its core was a sense of 'the personal, the concrete, the local' (Hoggart 1957, p.33). I would suggest that these three themes are in fact encapsulated by the one concept of 'home'. How did utility and the furniture shown at Britain Can Make It appeal to the people's deep sense of 'home'? Comments such as that of a of a 'decorator's wife', recorded by Mass Observation, sum up the situation: 'I have old-fashioned notions but I prefer my own home to anything I've seen. Some of the designs for the furniture look very cold, and too straight.'

Public resistance to 'modern design' was clearly not simply a dislike of the new. It was more the fact that this particular form of 'the new' went against a cultural attachment to a way of life. Change itself was not the problem. The election of the Labour Party and the enthusiasm with which the Beveridge Plan was received prove this. The crucial difference between these changes and those proposed by the design reformers was that the latter demanded change in a set of values. To this the public would not agree.

In terms of what Gordon Russell and others envisaged, utility furniture failed. The resilient spirit which had been the champion of the Home Front campaign also proved strong enough to resist all attempts, however well meaning, to alter a way of life in the post-war period. If habits in furniture buying did change at this time, it was due to the organic process of a younger generation reacting to the tastes of its parents.

In the end this lack of success hardly mattered; which was the more important, that the Beveridge Plan be implemented or that the public could recognize an Ercol chair? In any case, the Utility Scheme had served its real purpose – the provision of quality goods for those who needed them most at accessible prices – and had done so remarkably well. And, whether or not public taste moved on to a higher plane, utility had instilled a widespread awareness of design as a valid professional practice. Probably not much more could ever have reasonably been expected; a comment made by Paul Nash in *Weekend Review* in 1932 was as true for the 1940s as it was for the pre-war years: 'But the public who walk the streets looking into the windows and up at the buildings or those who listen to talks on the radio or read magazines must surely wonder what it is all about. "Modernistic," they murmur, and leave it at that.'

BIBLIOGRAPHY

PRIMARY SOURCES

Reports

Board of Trade   *Industrial Organisation and Development Act, 1947.*

Proposals for a Development Council of the Furniture Industry, HMSO, 1948.

Report by the Committee appointed by the Board of Trade under the chairmanship of Lord Gorell on the production and exhibition of articles of good design of everyday use, HMSO, 1932.

Design Digest   News From the Council of Industrial Design, *Report of the Furniture Working Party,* January 1947.

Furniture Development Council   *First Annual Report,* 1949.

Council for Art and Industry   *The Working Class Home: Its Furnishing and Equipment,* HMSO, May 1937.

Hansard Parliamentary Debates   *The Council of Industrial Design, House of Commons Official Report,* 19 December 1944.

Documents

Abbreviations   BL – British Library
NAL – National Art Library Archive of Art and Design.

PRO – Public Record Office.

BL BS 80/1	Council of Industrial Design, Annual Reports, 1945–47.
BL BS 80/9	*Design at Work. An Introduction to the Industrial Designer with a study of his methods of working and the position he holds in British Industry,* 1948.
NAL AAD 4-1977	Britain Can Make It, minutes from organizational meetings, 1945–46.
NAL AAD 11-1986	Clarke Furniture Archive.
PRO BT 54	British Industries Fair, minutes from meetings, 1946–51.
PRO BT 57 1	Council for Art and Industry, minutes of first meeting, 30 January 1934.
PRO BT 57 31	Council for Art and Industry, committee meeting minutes, July 1938–August 1939.
PRO BT 264 1	Furniture Development Council, minutes of meetings for 1949.
PRO RG 23 164	The Social Survey, *Utility and the Public, An enquiry made for the Board of Trade,* September – October 1950.
PRO RG 23 73	The Social Survey, *Utility Furniture, An enquiry made for the Board of Trade in association with the Council of Industrial Design,* May 1945.
PRO BT 131 61	Reconstruction Committee, minutes from the fortnightly meetings, January 1943 – April 1946.
PRO BT 131 64	Reconversion and Expansion of Civil Trade, monthly reports 1945–46.
PRO BT 183	Utility Furniture Drawings.

SECONDARY SOURCES

Banham, R., *Theory and Design in the First Machine Age*, Architectural Press, London, 1960.

Barnett, C., *The Audit of War, The Illusion and Reality of Britain as a Great Nation*, Macmillan, London, 1986.

Barrett, H. and Phillips, J., *Suburban Style, The British Home, 1840–1960*, MacDonald Orbis, London and Sydney, 1987.

Baynes, K. and K., *Gordon Russell*, Design Council, London, 1986.

Bertram, A., *The House, A Machine for Living In*, A & C Black, London, 1935.

Bertram, A., *Design in Daily Life*, A & C Black, London, 1937.

Blomfield, R., *Modernismus*, Macmillan, London, 1934.

Braithwaite, B., Davis, G. and Walsh, N. (eds), *Ragtime to Wartime, The Best of Good-Housekeeping, 1922–1939*, Ebury Press, London, 1986.

Brutton, M., 'Utility', *Design*, September 1974.

Calder, A., *The People's War, Britain 1939–1945*, Jonathan Cape, London, 1969.

Calder, A. and Sheridan, D. (eds), *Speak for Yourself, A Mass Observation Anthology, 1937–1949*, Jonathan Cape, London, 1984.

Carrington, N., *Design in the Home*, Bodley Head, London, 1935.

Chapman, D., *The Home and Social Status*, Routledge & Kegan Paul, London, 1935.

Cole, A. S. and H. K., *Fifty Years of the Public Work of Sir Henry Cole*, Chiswick Press, London, 1884.

Connell, A. D. and Blomfield, R., 'For and Against Modern Architecture', *The Listener*, 28 November 1934.

Council of Industrial Design, '*Britain Can Make It*', Supplement to the Board of Trade Journal, London, 1946. *Design '46*, Survey of British Industrial Design as Displayed at the 'Britain Can Make It' exhibition, London, 1946.

De La Valette, J., *The Conquest of Ugliness*, Methuen, London, 1935.

Design and Industries Association, DIA Yearbook, 1945–46.

Feaver, W., 'Art at the time', in *Thirties: British Art and Design before the War*, Arts Council, 1980.

Forty, A., *Objects of Desire; Design and Society, 1750–1980*, Thames & Hudson, 1986.

Geffrye Museum, *Utility Furniture and Fashion, 1941–1951*, ILEA, London, 1974.

Gloag, J., 'Design in the Festival', in *Design*, April 1951.

Hargreaves, E. L. and Gowing, M. M., *Civil Industry and Trade, The History of the Second World War*, HMSO and Longmans Green, London, 1952.

Harrison, C., *English Art and Modernism, 1900–1939*, Allen Lane, London, 1981.

Harrison, T. and Madge, C. (eds), *War Begins at Home*, Chatto & Windus, London, 1943.

Hoggart, R., *The Uses of Literacy*, Penguin Books, London, 1957.

Hooper, J., *Modern Furnishings and Fittings*, Batsford, London, 1948.

Joel, D., *The Adventure of British Furniture*, Ernest Benn, London, 1953.

Lambourne, L., *Utopian Craftsmen*, Astragal Books, London, 1980.

Lancaster, O., *A Cartoon History of Architecture*, John Murray, London, 1975.

Le Corbusier, *Towards a New Architecture*, John Rodker, London, 1927.

Le Corbusier, *The City of Tomorrow*, John Rodker, London, 1929.

Logie, G., *Furniture from Machines*, George Allen & Unwin, London, 1948.

Longmate, N., *How We Lived Then, A History of Everyday Life During the Second World War*, Hutchinson, London, 1971.

Love, G. H., *The Pan Book of Woodwork*, Longmans Green, London, 1958.

Lowndes, I., *The Silent Revolution*, OUP, Oxford, 1937.

MacDonald and Porter, *'Putting on the Style', Setting Up Home in the 1950s*, Geffrye Museum, 1990.

Marwick, A., *The Home Front, Britain and the Second World War*, Thames & Hudson, London, 1976.

Morris, L. and Radford, R., *The Story of the AIA*, MOMA, Oxford, 1983.

Morton, A. L. (ed), *The Political Writings of William Morris*, Lawrence & Wishart, London, 1973.

Nash, P., 'Going Modern and Being British', *The Weekend Review*, 12 March 1932.

O'Morgan, K., *Labour in Power*, OUP, Oxford and New York, 1984.

Patmore, D., *Modern Furnishing and Decoration*, The Studio, London and New York, 1936.

Prus, T. and Dawson, D., *A New Design for Living, Design in British Interiors 1930–1957*, Lane Publications, London, 1982.

Russell, G., 'Taste in Design', in *Art and Industry*, August 1944.

Russell, G., *The Things We See; Furniture*, Drayton, London, 1947.

Russell, G., *Design at Work*, Council of Industrial Design, 1948.

Russell, G., 'How to buy Furniture', in *Ideal Home Yearbook, 1953–1954*.

Russell, G., *The Designer's Trade, An Autobiography*, George Allen & Unwin, London, 1968.

Sparke, P. (ed), 'The Furniture Retailer as Taste Maker', in *Did Britain Make It? British Design In Context, 1946–1986*, Design Council, London, 1986.

Stevenson, J., *British Society, 1914–1945*, Penguin Books, London, 1984.

Stevenson, J. and Cook, C., *The Slump, Society and Politics During the Depression*, Jonathan Cape, London, 1977.

Walker, J. A., *Design History and the History of Design*, Pluto Press, London, 1989.

Ward, N., *Home in the '20s and '30s*, Ian Allan, London, 1978.

Unpublished material

Cohen, J. H., *William Morris and Utopia, News from Nowhere*, 1986.

Channon, A., *R. D. Russell, Designer for Industry, 1930–1935*, V&A/RCA MA thesis, 1984.

Warden, S., *Furniture for the Living Room, An Investigation of the Interaction between Society, Industry and Design in Britain from 1919–1939*, PhD thesis, Brighton Polytechnic, 1980.

Periodicals

Architectural Review, 1946–1951.

Art and Industry, 1940–1950.

The Cabinet Maker and Complete Home Furnisher, 1941–1951.

Design, 1940–1951.

Picture Post, 1939–1952.

Utility Furniture Catalogue
1943

INTRODUCTION

by the

Rt. Hon. Hugh Dalton, P.C., M.P.

President of the Board of Trade.

THIS booklet describes and illustrates the first edition of utility furniture. In extending utility production to this new field, my aim is to provide, for those who really need it, furniture which is sound in construction, agreeable in design and reasonable in price. Materials available for furniture-making are to-day very scarce, but, as these pages show, the designers have done their job well. Mr. Charles Tennyson, the Chairman of my Advisory Committee, and his colleagues, have devoted much time and many valuable ideas to this interesting new venture.

Hugh Dalton.

LIVING ROOM

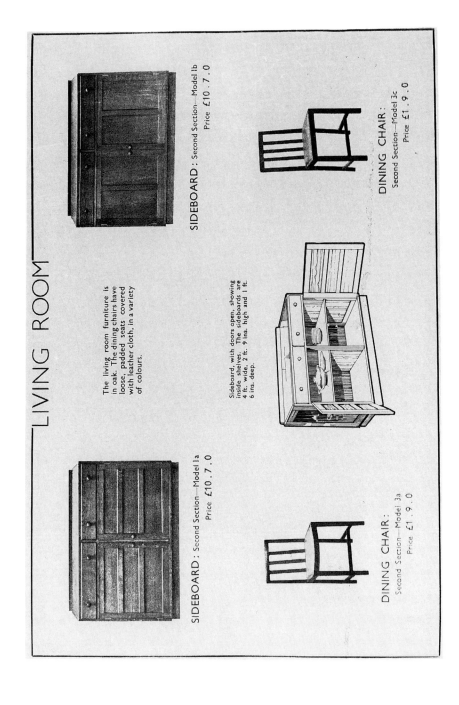

The living room furniture is in oak. The dining chairs have loose, padded seats covered with leather cloth, in a variety of colours.

Sideboard, with doors open, showing inside shelves. The sideboards are 4 ft. wide, 2 ft. 9 ins. high and 1 ft. 6 ins. deep.

SIDEBOARD : Second Section—Model 1b
Price £10 . 7 . 0

DINING CHAIR :
Second Section—Model 3c
Price £1 . 9 . 0

SIDEBOARD : Second Section—Model 1a
Price £10 . 7 . 0

DINING CHAIR :
Second Section—Model 3a
Price £1 . 9 . 0

LIVING ROOM

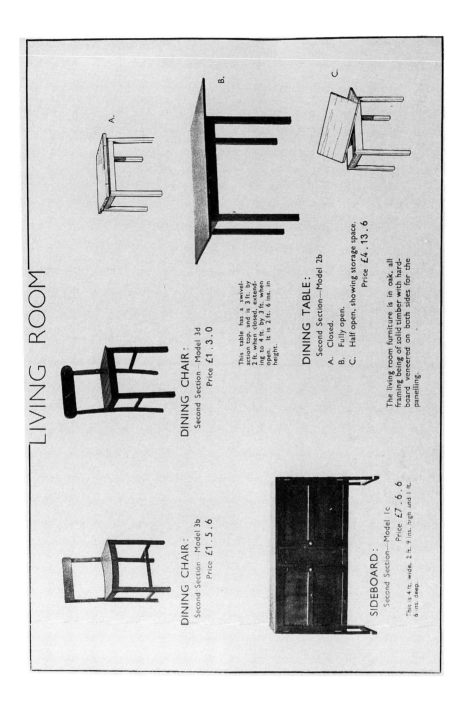

A.

B.

C.

DINING CHAIR:
Second Section—Model 3d
Price £1 . 3 . 0

DINING TABLE:
Second Section—Model 2b

A. Closed.
B. Fully open.
C. Half open, showing storage space.
Price £4 . 13 . 6

This table has a swivel-action top, and is 3 ft. by 2 ft. when closed, extending to 4 ft. by 3 ft. when open. It is 2 ft. 6 ins. in height.

The living room furniture is in oak, all framing being of solid timber with hardboard veneered on both sides for the panelling.

DINING CHAIR:
Second Section Model 3b
Price £1 . 5 . 6

SIDEBOARD:
Second Section—Model 1c
Price £7 . 6 . 6

This is 4 ft. wide, 2 ft. 9 ins. high and 1 ft. 6 ins. deep.

BEDROOM

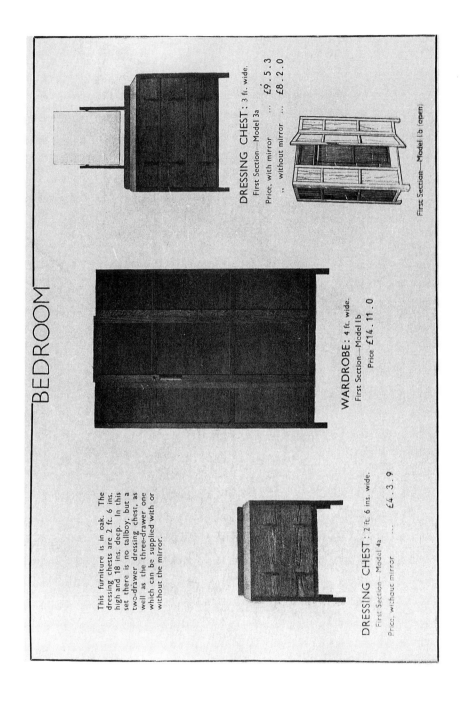

This furniture is in oak. The dressing chests are 2 ft. 6 ins. high and 18 ins. deep. In this set there is no tallboy, but a two-drawer dressing chest, as well as the three-drawer one which can be supplied with or without the mirror.

DRESSING CHEST : 3 ft. wide.
First Section—Model 3a
Price, with mirror .... £9 . 5 . 3
„ without mirror .... £8 . 2 . 0

First Section—Model 1b (open)

WARDROBE : 4 ft. wide.
First Section—Model 1b
Price £14 . 11 . 0

DRESSING CHEST : 2 ft. 6 ins. wide.
First Section—Model 4a
Price, without mirror .... £4 . 3 . 9

BEDROOM

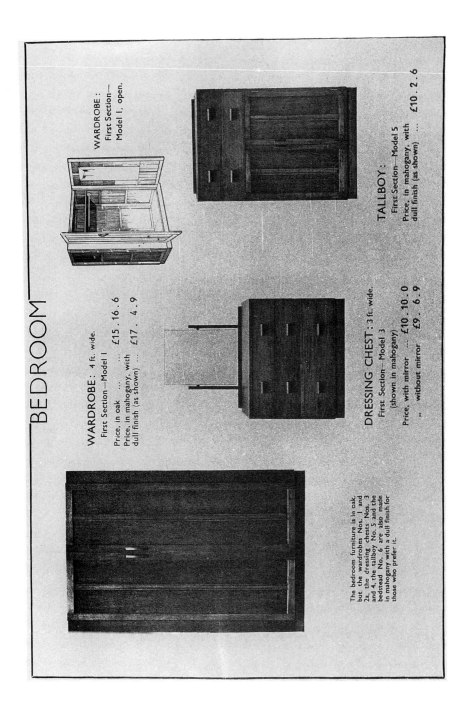

WARDROBE: First Section— Model I, open.

WARDROBE: 4 ft. wide.
First Section—Model I
Price, in oak ... ... £15 . 16 . 6
Price, in mahogany, with dull finish (as shown) ... £17 . 4 . 9

DRESSING CHEST: 3 ft. wide.
First Section—Model 3
(shown in mahogany)
Price, with mirror ... £10 . 10 . 0
" without mirror ... £9 . 6 . 9

TALLBOY:
First Section—Model 5
Price, in mahogany, with dull finish (as shown) ... £10 . 2 . 6

The bedroom furniture is in oak, but the wardrobes Nos. I and 2a, the dressing chests Nos. 3 and 4, the tallboy No. 5 and the bedstead No. 6 are also made in mahogany with a dull finish for those who prefer it.

The dressing chests are made in 3 ft. and 2 ft. 6 ins. sizes and they can be supplied, if desired, without the mirror, so providing an alternative low chest model. The chests are 2 ft. 6 ins. high and 18 ins. deep.

DRESSING CHEST: 2 ft. 6 ins. wide.

First Section—Model 4

	Prices
In oak, with mirror ...	£8 . 11 . 0
In oak, without mirror	£7 . 11 . 0
In mahogany, with mirror ...	£9 . 4 . 0
In mahogany, without mirror	£8 . 4 . 0

WARDROBE: 3 ft. wide.

First Section—Model 2a

Price, in oak	...	£13 . 2 . 9
„ in mahogany	...	£14 . 0 . 0

TALLBOY:

First Section Model 5

Price, in oak, as shown £9 . 5 . 3

Interior view of tallboy. All the tallboys have two drawers above and a cupboard with a shelf below. They are 2 ft. 9 ins. wide, 4 ft. high and 1 ft. 6 ins. deep.

BEDROOM

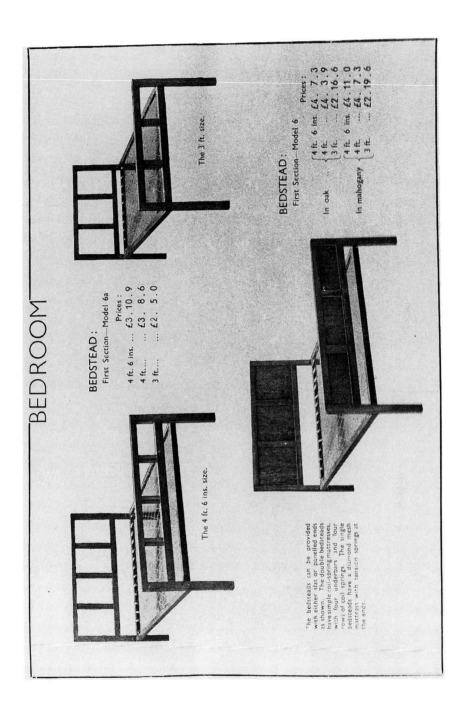

BEDSTEAD:

First Section—Model 6a

Prices :

4 ft. 6 ins.	£3 . 10 . 9
4 ft.	£3 . 8 . 6
3 ft.	£2 . 5 . 0

The 4 ft. 6 ins. size.

The 3 ft. size.

BEDSTEAD:

First Section—Model 6

Prices :

In oak	4 ft. 6 ins.	£4 . 7 . 3
	4 ft.	£4 . 3 . 9
	3 ft.	£2 . 16 . 6
In mahogany	4 ft. 6 ins.	£4 . 11 . 0
	4 ft.	£4 . 7 . 3
	3 ft.	£2 . 19 . 6

The bedsteads can be provided with either slat or panelled ends as shown. The double bedsteads have simple coil-spring mattresses, with four underbars and four rows of coil springs. The single bedsteads have a diamond mesh mattress with tension springs at the ends.

99

KITCHEN

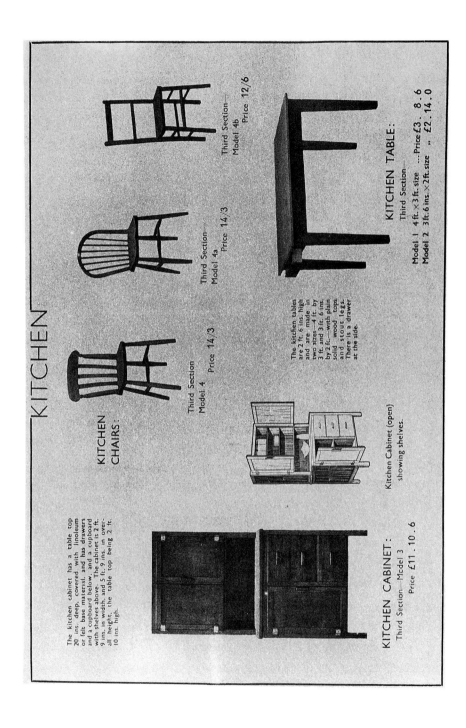

KITCHEN CHAIRS:

Third Section—
Model 4   Price 14/3

Third Section—
Model 4a   Price 14/3

Third Section—
Model 4b   Price 12/6

KITCHEN TABLE:

Third Section—

Model 1 4 ft. × 3 ft. size ... Price £3 . 8 . 6
Model 2 3 ft. 6 ins. × 2 ft. size " £2 . 14 . 0

The kitchen tables are 2 ft. 6 ins. high and are made in two sizes—4 ft. by 3 ft. and 3 ft. 6 ins. by 2 ft.—with plain solid wood tops and stout legs. There is a drawer at the side.

Kitchen Cabinet (open) showing shelves.

KITCHEN CABINET:

Third Section—Model 3

Price £11 . 10 . 6

The kitchen cabinet has a table top 20 ins. deep, covered with linoleum or felt base material, and has drawers and a cupboard below, and a cupboard with shelves above. The cabinet is 2 ft. 9 ins. in width, and 5 ft. 9 ins. in over-all height, the table top being 2 ft. 10 ins. high.

100

NURSERY

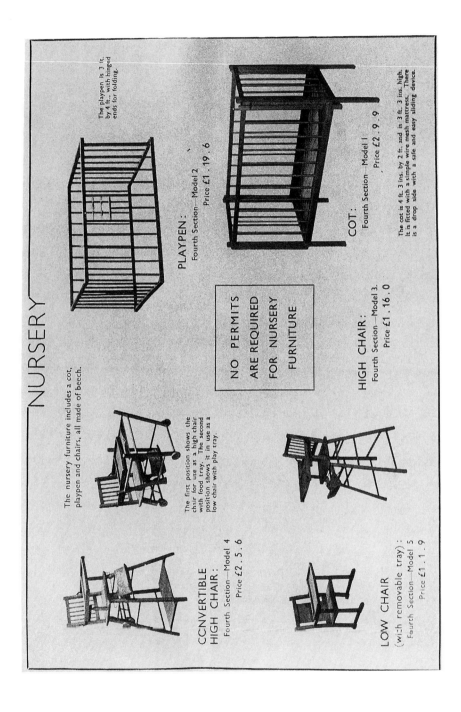

The playpen is 3 ft. by 4 ft., with hinged ends for folding.

PLAYPEN:
Fourth Section—Model 2
Price £1.19.6

COT:
Fourth Section—Model 1
Price £2.9.9

The cot is 4 ft. 3 ins. by 2 ft. and is 3 ft. 3 ins. high. It is fitted with a simple wire mesh mattress. There is a drop side with a safe and easy sliding device.

NO PERMITS ARE REQUIRED FOR NURSERY FURNITURE

HIGH CHAIR:
Fourth Section—Model 3.
Price £1.16.0

The nursery furniture includes a cot, playpen and chairs, all made of beech.

The first position shows the chair for use as a high chair with food tray. The second position shows it in use as a low chair with play tray.

CONVERTIBLE HIGH CHAIR:
Fourth Section—Model 4
Price £2.5.6

LOW CHAIR
(with removable tray):
Fourth Section—Model 5
Price £1.1.9

101

MISCELLANEOUS

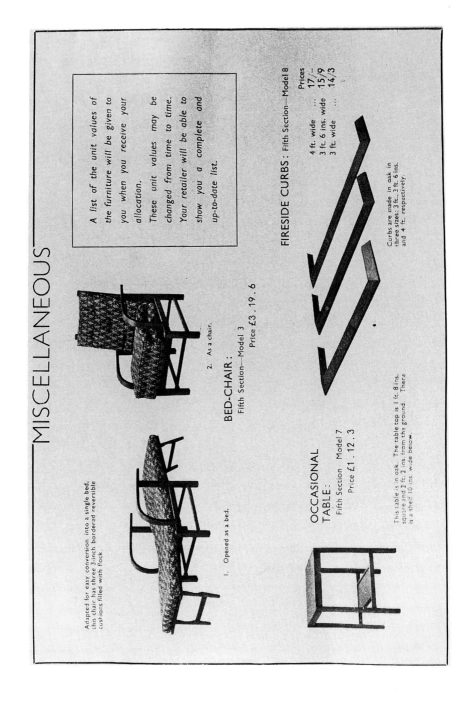

A list of the unit values of the furniture will be given to you when you receive your allocation.

These unit values may be changed from time to time. Your retailer will be able to show you a complete and up-to-date list.

Adapted for easy conversion into a single bed, this chair has three 3-inch bordered reversible cushions filled with flock.

1. Opened as a bed.

2. As a chair.

BED-CHAIR:
Fifth Section—Model 3

Price £3 . 19 . 6

FIRESIDE CURBS: Fifth Section—Model 8

		Prices
4 ft. wide	....	17/—
3 ft. 6 ins. wide	....	15/9
3 ft. wide	....	14/3

Curbs are made in oak in three sizes: 3 ft. 3 ft. 6 ins. and 4 ft. respectively.

OCCASIONAL TABLE:
Fifth Section: Model 7

Price £1 . 12 . 3

This table is in oak. The table top is 1 ft. 8 ins. square and 2 ft. 2 ins. from the ground. There is a shelf 10 ins. wide below.

INDEX

Addison, Paul 37
Aesthetic thinking 25
Antelope chair 51
Artists' International Association 31
Arts and Crafts movement 20, 23, 25–7,
  31, 33, 36, 80, 81, 83
Attlee, Clement 3, 26, 38, 80

Barnett, Correlli, 23, 81
Bathrooms 70
Bauhaus refugees 31
Bedroom furniture 71
Bevan, Aneurin 21
Beveridge Plan 84
Beveridge Report 21
Beveridge, W.H. 37
Black, Misha 36, 37
Blomfield, Reginald 17
Board of Trade 3, 10, 21, 23, 35, 38, 39,
  43, 45, 56, 59, 71, 80, 82, 83
Britain Can Make It (BCMI) exhibition 41–
  3, 45, 50, 51, 55, 61, 67–71, 73, 83, 84
British Art in Industry 35
British Industries Fair 35, 41
British Institute of Industrial Art 35
Britishness 27

Cabinet Maker, The 19, 59, 83
Central Prices Regulation Committee
  (CPRC) 5
Chapman, Denis 79
Chiltern range 17
Clarke, Maurice 61, 62
Clinch, Edwin 7, 11, 14, 27, 37
Cole, Henry 26, 28, 29, 33
Collectivism, 36, 82
Communism 21, 31
Conran, Terence 52
Contemporary style 51, 55
Costs 11, 14, 72
Cotswold range 19
Council for Art and Industry (CAI) 29,
  34–6, 38, 39, 68
Council of Industrial Design (CoID) 29,
  39–41, 43, 45, 50, 51, 55, 56, 67, 69–
  73, 77, 78
Cripps, Stafford 3, 7, 21, 42, 44, 50
Cutler, H.T. 7, 11

Dalton, Hugh 3, 5, 7, 23, 32, 38, 39, 43
Decoration 11, 32, 64
Denby, Elizabeth 5, 63
Depression 34
Design 52
Design and Industries Association (DIA)
  29, 68, 73, 75
Design at Work 51
Design Centre 39
Design Council 29
Design reform 14–21
Design Research Unit 38
Design specifications 5
Deutsch Werkbund 31
Did Britain Make It? 77
Distribution 14
Dockets 7

Economic growth 34
Eighteenth-century furniture 55
Environment 32
Ercol chair 45, 50
European Modern Movement 29
European modernism 81
Exports 42–3

Festival of Britain 29–41, 51, 55
Fitness for purpose 17, 29, 31
Freedom of Design 7, 44, 62
Furniture, choice of 78
Furniture Development Council (FDC) 7,
  40
Furniture trade
  and government intervention 59–66
  and modernism 63

and socialism 61, 83
and utility furniture 63–4
political affiliations of 83

Geffrye Museum 77
Gloag, John 5, 52, 55, 64
'Good design' criteria 17, 51
Gothicism 25
Government intervention 59
Great Exhibition of 1851 29, 82

Harrison, Tom 16–17
High Wycombe 61
Hire purchase 77
Hoggart, Richard 83
Hollywood Deco 14
Home Front campaign 4, 9, 37, 84
Honesty 25, 27

Industrial design 38–40

Jenkinson, Charles 7
Joel, David 62
Johnstone, W. 5
Journal of Design and Manufacture 29

Keynesianism 37
Kitchens 69–70

Labour Party 21–4, 34, 37, 44, 45, 55, 61,
    67, 83, 84
Labour-saving gadgets 70
Lancaster, Osbert 14–15
Lebus, Herman 7
Le Corbusier 17, 32
Left Book Club 21
Licences 5, 10, 40
Living standards 4
Llewellyn, William 35

Make or Mar? 75
Marxism 21
Mass Observation 17, 68, 73, 84
Mass production 20, 27, 39
Ministry of Supply 10
Modern design, public resistance to 84
Modern fittings 70
Modern furniture 70
Modern Movement 20
Modern styles 68
Modernism 17, 26, 29, 31, 33, 63, 81
Morality 25

Morris, William 20, 24–7, 36, 54, 81
Morrison, Herbert 38, 55

Nash, Paul 84
National Exhibition 29
National Register of Industrial Art
    Designers 35
Nature of Gothic, The 26
New Statesman 21

Ornamentation 11

Penalties 62
Pick, Frank 35, 39
Plywood supplies 11
Policy Committee of NEC 23
Popular taste 70–1
Price control 73
Prices of Goods Act 62
Pritchard, Jack 40
Public reaction 67–84
Public resistance to modern design 84
Pugin, A.N.W. 25, 26
Putting On The Style – Setting Up Home In
    The 1950s 77

Quality control 40, 62, 72

Race, Ernest 51
Rationing 7
Reconstruction Committee 38, 40, 44
Reconversion of Civil Industry 62
Redgrave, Richard 29
Register Your Choice 73, 78
Reid, A.L. 15
Reproductive excesses 51
Retailer as taste-maker 77
Royal College of Art 28
Ruskin, John 24, 26, 54, 81
Russell, Gordon 7, 19, 21, 27, 28, 32, 34,
    36, 40, 44, 45, 50, 51, 63, 68, 71, 77,
    78, 80, 84

Second World War 21, 37, 82
Simplicity 25, 27, 51, 73
Social planning 4
Social policy 3, 4
Social pressure 78
Socialism 61, 80, 83
Socialist ideology 82
Society of Arts 28
Sparke, Penny 77

INDEX

Standard Emergency Furniture 5
Standardized design 61
Steel furniture 68
Stones of Venice, The 26, 27

Technocracy 37, 38
Tennyson, Charles 5
Timber
  allocation 3
  consumption 3
  quotas 11
  rationing 3
  shortages 40
  supplies 10
Timber Control Department 10
Traditional style 69, 70
Transport 14

Unemployment, reduction of 4
Uses of Literacy, The 83
Utility Advisory Committee 20
'Utility and the Public', reaction of general
  public to 72
Utility Furniture Advisory Committee
  (UFAC) 5, 7, 11, 19, 37, 62

Utility Furniture (Making and Supply)
  (Revocation) Order 7
Utility mark CC41 5, 61
Utility Scheme 11, 21, 36–40, 44, 51, 59,
  61–3
  abandonment of 73
  demise of 7–9
  origins 3
  principle of 3
  purpose of 84
  reaction of general public to 72

Victoria and Albert Museum 28

Walton, Alan 50
War socialism 3, 34, 36, 37
Weekend Review 84
Welsford, V. 7
Winborn, E. 7
Windsor chair 45
Working class culture 83
'Working Class Home; Its Furnishing and
  Equipment' 37

Zoning 14, 61